Slobodan Milosevic on Trial

A COMPANION

Michael P. Scharf

William A. Schabas

Continuum

New York London

2002

The Continuum International Publishing Group Inc
370 Lexington Avenue, New York, NY 10017

The Continuum International Publishing Company Ltd
The Tower Building, 11 York Road, London SE1 7NX

Library of Congress Cataloging-in-Publication Data

Scharf, Michael P., 1963–
    Slobodan Milosevic on trial: a companion/Michael P. Scharf, William A. Schabas.
        p. cm.
Includes bibliographical references and index.
    ISBN 0-8264-1411-7
    1. Miloséviâc, Slobodan, 1941—Trials, litigation, etc. 2. Trials (Crimes against humanity)—Netherlands—Hague. I. Miloséviâc, Slobodan, 1941– II. Schabas, William, 1950– III. Title.
    KZ1203.M55 S33 2002
    341.6'9—dc21

                                                                2001008544

CONTENTS

ABOUT THE AUTHORS

Michael Scharf

During the George H.W. Bush and Clinton administrations, Michael Scharf served in the Office of the Legal Adviser of the United States Department of State, where he held the positions of counsel to the Counter-Terrorism Bureau, attorney-adviser for law enforcement and intelligence, attorney-adviser for United Nations affairs, and delegate to the United Nations General Assembly and to the United Nations Human Rights Commission. In 1993 Scharf was awarded the State Department's Meritorious Honor Award "in recognition of superb performance and exemplary leadership in support of U.S. policy initiatives regarding the former Yugoslavia." Scharf left the State Department in August 1993 to join the faculty of the New England School of Law in Boston, where he served as professor of law and director of the Center for International Law and Policy. In 2002 Scharf joined the faculty of Case Western Reserve University School of Law as professor of law and director of the Cox Center International War Crimes Research Office.

Scharf is the author of numerous articles and several books about international criminal law, including *Balkan Justice,* which was nominated for the Pulitzer Prize in 1998, and *The International Criminal Tribunal for Rwanda,* which was awarded the American Society of International Law's Certificate of Merit for the outstanding book in international law in 1999. Since 1996 Scharf has served as a consultant to the Office of the Prosecutor of the International Tribunal and, under a program sponsored by a Soros Foundation grant, he and his students have provided the international prosecutor with over one hundred research memoranda on issues pending before the International Tribunal. He has testified as an expert before the U.S. Senate Foreign Relations Committee and has frequently appeared as a commentator on CNN, Fox News, Court TV, the BBC, and National Public Radio.

William A. Schabas

William A. Schabas is director of the Irish Center for Human Rights at the National University of Ireland, Galway, where he also holds the professorship in human rights law. Prior to assuming this position in 2000, he was professor of human rights law and criminal law, and dean of the faculty of law at the University of Quebec, Montreal, Canada. He has been a visiting professor at several universities in France and has lectured throughout the world. He is a member of the Quebec Bar and practised law for many years before many of Canada's major courts, including the Supreme Court of Canada and the Quebec Court of Appeal, in the fields of criminal law, administrative law, and civil law. He was a member of the Quebec Human Rights Tribunal from 1996 to 2000. Professor Schabas was a senior fellow at the United States Institute of Peace in Washington during the academic year 1998-1999.

A former journalist, Professor Schabas is the author of over one hundred academic articles and twelve books, including *Introduction to the International Criminal Court* (2001), *Genocide in International Law* (2000), and *The Abolition of the Death Penalty in International Law* (1997). Professor Schabas has also participated in international human rights missions to Rwanda, Burundi, Chechnya, South Africa, Kenya, Uganda, Sudan, Cambodia, and Guyana. He has also served as a consultant to the Ministry of Justice of Rwanda, the U.S. Agency for International Development, and the Organization for Security and Cooperation in Europe, and he was a delegate to the 1988 Rome Diplomatic Conference for the Establishment of an International Criminal Court.

CHAPTER 1

Introduction

Slobodan Milosevic. Derided by the West as the "Butcher of the Balkans." From 1991 to 1999 his troops fought four brutal Balkan wars. Hundreds of thousands died, most of them innocent civilians, and millions were displaced. Milosevic saw himself as a modern-day Abe Lincoln, employing force in a valiant effort to hold his crumbling Yugoslavia together. It is now alleged, however, that the Serb leader's tactics included systematic war crimes and ethnic cleansing. These ultimately prompted the United States and its North Atlantic Treaty Organization (NATO) allies to initiate a controversial bombing campaign in the spring of 1999 to halt the bloodshed in Kosovo.

Soon after his military defeat Milosevic fell from power in the face of a popular revolt. Now he faces international justice before the United Nations–created International Criminal Tribunal for the Former Yugoslavia (ICTY) in The Hague, Netherlands. His case number—IT-02-54—will live in infamy. Milosevic is the first former head of state ever to face international justice, and he is charged with the most horrific crimes known to mankind: grave breaches of the Geneva Conventions, violations of the laws or customs of war, crimes against humanity, and genocide.

Milosevic has been charged in three separate indictments, each dealing with a distinct war in the violent history of the territory of the former Yugoslavia during the 1990s. Chronologically, the first indictment deals with the war in Croatia that raged during the final months of 1991. Croatia had declared its independence from Yugoslavia, and forces commanded by Belgrade fought to carve off portions of the new state so that they could be eventually incorporated within a "Greater Serbia." Charges against Milosevic in this indictment address a range of crimes aimed at "ethnically cleansing" Croats from regions of their country where there was a significant Serb population. Charges relating to the brutal and destructive sieges of Vukovar and Dubrovnik are at the heart of the indictment.

The second indictment concerns the war in Bosnia and Herzegovina (Bosnia), which began in April 1992, following its secession from Yugoslavia, and continued until the Dayton Peace Agreement, in late 1995. In other trials the ICTY has already established that Bosnian Serb forces were responsible for a range of atrocities directed against Croat and Muslim populations, including the appalling massacre of seven thousand civilians at Srebrenica in July 1995. Milosevic was not in direct command, as he would be in Kosovo. The war appeared to be conducted by proxy forces under an autonomous Bosnian Serb leadership. The challenge for the prosecutor is to prove that there was a chain of command and influence running back to Belgrade.

The third indictment deals with Kosovo over the first six months of 1999. An increasingly vigorous secessionist campaign in what is today still part of Yugoslavia challenged the Belgrade government during the late 1990s. It was met by brutal repression from the central authorities and their representatives. As civil war escalated and civilians became hostage to the appalling violence, the Kosovo Albanian population—an overwhelming majority within the territory—fled from their homes to havens within Kosovo or in neighboring states. The ICTY prosecutor maintains that Milosevic and his forces pushed them out with a mixture of murder, pillage, and persecution.

Nobody suggests that Milosevic himself dirtied his hands and personally committed any of these atrocities. It is as a commander, leader, and organizer that his possible criminal liability arises. The prosecution confronts many of the problems that plague domestic prosecutions of organized crime figures. The prosecutor intends to demonstrate that there was a form of criminal conspiracy, or "joint criminal enterprise," of which Milosevic stood at the head. In the absence of documents or credible insiders, much of this must be done with circumstantial evidence. Alternatively, the prosecutor can fall back on a principle by which Milosevic, as a commander, can be held responsible for failing to prevent or punish crimes committed by his subordinates.

A conviction in this case may be more difficult to obtain than widely believed, in light of the unusual facts, governing rules, and guiding precedents. Milosevic has challenged the fairness of the proceedings and has sought to equate his actions in Kosovo with the post–September 11 American war on terrorism and its efforts to drive the Taliban and al-Qaeda from Afghanistan. He has indicated that he will summon former U.S. president Bill Clinton, secretary of state Madeleine Albright, Special Envoy Richard Holbrooke, British prime minister Tony Blair, and United Nations secretary-general Kofi Annan to prove he was a peacemaker rather than a war criminal.

The televised trial of Slobodan Milosevic is proving to be the world's most closely watched criminal proceeding since the case of O. J. Simpson, the American football player and movie star who was eventually acquitted of killing his wife and her friend. Case number IT-02-54 will be the most important international trial since the Nazi leaders were judged at Nuremberg in 1945 and 1946.

This book is designed to play a role similar to the program guide at a major sporting event, informing the reader what to watch for, who the players are, what the rules are, who won in the past, and who is likely to win now. This comprehensive guide to the Milosevic trial includes a chronology of events that led up to the monumental proceeding, biographies of the trial participants, an explanation of the governing law and rules of procedure, an analysis of the merits of the case, and a glossary of the key legal terms and concepts that are at the heart of this unprecedented trial.

The authors have been deeply involved in international justice issues since the International Criminal Tribunal for the Former Yugoslavia was established and even before, participating in its creation, then observing and commenting upon its evolution. It is our hope that this book will render the Milosevic trial comprehensible to the public and educate readers about the increasingly important field of international criminal law. The reader will note that diacritical marks to Serbo-Croatian names have been omitted in the text for uniformity and ease of reading. The authors are grateful to Anna M. Haughton for her research assistance. We dedicate this book to the people of the former Yugoslavia in the hope that the Milosevic trial will contribute to restoring peace for that troubled part of the world.

CHAPTER 2

The Rise of Slobodan Milosevic

In *Eichmann in Jerusalem*, political philosopher Hannah Arendt described staring at Adolf Eichmann day after day during his trial in an effort to perceive evil. Instead, she found the genocidal Nazi "terrifyingly ordinary." Observers at the Nuremberg trial of the Nazi leadership reported the defendants, with one or two exceptions, as petty, squabbling men. But Slobodan Milosevic seems destined to leave a somewhat different impression. In his initial appearances before the International Criminal Tribunal for the former Yugoslavia (ICTY) he has been combative and sly, with a gift for judicial repartee and the ruses of an able advocate.

Yet stripped of the trappings of power, Milosevic does not come across as the brilliant "silver fox" described in American negotiator Richard Holbrooke's memoir. Nor is he the charismatic leader able to whip his followers into a nationalist fury in the style of Adolf Hitler, as Vice President Al Gore once suggested. Rather, the sixty-year-old former Serb president looks the part of a drab government functionary, with a stocky build, receding hairline, pouting lip, and sagging jowls. Indeed, prior to his meteoric rise to power in the 1980s, Milosevic was known as an easygoing apparatchik who knew how to work the system but lacked any apparent grand political ambitions. If not for his association with two people—his ambitious wife, Mirjana Markovic, and his politically connected law school classmate Ivan Stambolic—the world might never have known the name *Slobodan Milosevic*.

A Childhood of Tragedy and Isolation

Slobodan Milosevic was born in Pozarevac, Serbia, to Svetozar and Stanislava Milosevic on August 22, 1941, at the height of the Nazi occupation of Yugoslavia. The small town of Pozarevac, located a few miles south of the Yugoslav capital, Belgrade, is linked through name and reputation with a nearby nineteenth-century prison. Although Slobodan was surely too young to fully comprehend the turmoil around him—the resistance to fascist occupation and local collaborators, the struggle for food and shelter, the omnipresent Nazi cruelties—his life was greatly affected by the turbulent times.

Milosevic's mother, Stanislava, a schoolteacher and dedicated communist activist, sought to pass onto Slobodan and his older brother her strong beliefs. These convictions were not, however, shared by their father, Svetozar, who abandoned the family a few years after Slobodan's birth, leaving Stanislava to raise her sons alone. The breakdown of the marriage was humiliating and traumatic and gave the local gossips in the provincial Serbian town much to discuss.

Slobodan is said to have been a solitary child. Patterns of abandonment surrounded the young Milosevic and could be seen as factors in the formation of a hardened, isolated individual. In his early years he struggled academically. His stocky frame did not lend itself to athletic endeavors. Slobodan grew up in a united Yugoslavia under Josip Broz Tito. He was influenced by the atmosphere of elitism and partisan hero worship, becoming a somewhat pedantic communist conformist. It was in his high school years that Slobodan began to excel academically and to attract the attention of higher ups in the local Communist Party. It was also during this time that he met the young woman, named Mirjana Markovic, who would shape his destiny.

Both of Slobodan's parents ultimately committed suicide. Svetozar shot himself in 1962, when Slobodan was at University Law School in Belgrade. The investigation concluded that Svetozar was suffering from depression. Slobodan, then in his twenties, had had little contact with his father and made no comment to other students about the event, except to deny that it took place. His mother, Stanislava, followed suit thirty years later. In 1994, after a confrontation with Mirjana about the grandchildren, Stanislava hung herself.

Slobodan was said to have told a friend who aided in cutting down Stanislava's body, "My mother never forgave me for Mira."

Mira Markovic: Juliet or Lady MacBeth?

One cannot decipher Slobodan Milosevic without also focusing on his lifetime partner, Mirjana Markovic. They met while still in high school and immediately became sweethearts. Mirjana was not particularly attractive. She had a frumpy appearance, her doughy face punctured by dark eyes and framed by jet-black bangs. But Slobodan was intrigued by Mirjana's family history. She saw in him a vehicle for pursuing her political ambitions. Fellow classmates claim that "they were practically glued together." One of their biographers, Slavoljub Djukic, in *Milosevic and Markovic: A Lust For Power,* described the young couple's first meeting in the following terms:

> Snow had fallen. They stood exposed to the wind on a cold winter day, shivering, yet youthfully at ease. It was so touching. They learned that day that they were both exceedingly polite and well matched. From then on Mirjana feared neither cold nor darkness, nor mosquitoes. From that point on Slobodan would always stand by her, whether or not she was right.

Mirjana Markovic came to the relationship with her own troubled family history. Markovic's mother, Vera Miletic, was a notorious anti-Nazi resistance fighter who was labeled a traitor to the communist resistance upon her death. Vera discovered communism at Belgrade University and subsequently had an affair with a young partisan named Moma Markovic, who had already distinguished himself in the Communist Party. During the resistance in 1942, Vera gave birth to Mirjana in the small village of Brezane while hidden by a communist supporter. The infant was immediately sent off to be raised by Vera's parents in Pozarevac, while Vera returned to the communist resistance aimed at ousting the Germans.

Eight months later, Vera, who went by the *nom de guerre* Mira, was captured by the Nazis, tortured, and killed. Soon afterwards, the principal figures in the local communist underground were arrested and executed, leading to the belief that Vera had disclosed their names and locations during interrogation. In light of this perceived betrayal, Vera was labeled a coward and the most despised of turn-coats. Moma Markovic's own memoir condemned Vera as a traitor and stated that the proof lay in the Nazi police reports.

Nevertheless, Mirjana idolized her mother, even taking on Vera's code name, *Mira,* as her own name. In addition, Mirjana (now Mira) often wore a silk rose in her hair, a symbol her mother had used as a socialist emblem. Mira retained all of the items her mother knitted in prison as prized possessions. While Mira grew up venerating her deceased mother, her father, Moma Markovic, turned his back on his daughter and began a new family while rising to the uppermost echelons of power in communist Yugoslavia.

Reports vary as to Mira's relationship with her father. She would see him during summer visits to the island of Brioni, one of Tito's plushest resorts, where she would spend time with her father's new family. It is said that she intensely resented these visits, feeling like an outsider, and that her father did not formally recognize her as his kin until she was sixteen years old. Mira never forgave her father and stepmother and wound up suing her stepmother for her father's estate upon his death. Mira told her attorney that it was not the modest estate that interested her, for she planned to give it to charity, but revenge for how her mother's good name was blackened by her father.

Another of Mira's famous relatives was her maternal aunt, Davorjanka Paunovic, an extraordinarily beautiful but frail woman who during college became Tito's wartime secretary and mistress. Tito and Davorjanka lived together in the White Palace after the communists seized control of Belgrade, in 1944. When she died two years later of tuberculosis, a devastated Tito buried her just outside his bedroom window at the Palace.

Mira Markovic and Slobodan Milosevic found in each other a relationship of intense codependence. The external forces that affected each of the young adult's dysfunctional families was probably the cement that bonded these adolescents together in mutual determination to be recognized and attain power. Slobodan was fascinated by Mira's lineage. Mira found in Slobodan the instrument to reach her ambitious goals. These were stoked by her need to rehabilitate her mother's name and to live up to the pedigree of her elite communist family, by which she felt abandoned.

After high school, they attended university at Belgrade together. Slobodan studied law; Mira sociology. Slobodan graduated with a law degree in 1964, and the two were married the next year. Communist Party membership was the singular road to success in Yugoslavia during the 1960s. Slobodan had joined the Communist Party while in high school; Mira joined at university. They both became committed members and activists. In his biography of Mira, Serb author Slavoljub Djukic describes how Mira once pointed to a portrait of Tito, whose picture then adorned every public building, and remarked to a cousin that "Sloba's picture will one day hang like Tito's." Her cousin was taken aback: Slobodan did not seem the type to fulfill these grandiose aspirations. But Mira was certain. Although Slobodan had not yet begun his climb up the party ladder, he was busy learning the lessons of survival and political manipulation of which he would eventually become a master.

Connections as Stepping Stones

Slobodan Milosevic excelled in law school, and it was there that he made the most important connection of his life. Ivan Stambolic, five years Milosevic's senior, became his mentor and best friend and later blazed the path of success for Milosevic. Stambolic hailed from a politically powerful family. Although his parents had wished him to be an industrialist, Stambolic enrolled in the Belgrade law school while working the night shift in a motor factory. Petar Stambolic, Ivan's uncle, was one of the top officials in Yugoslavia, and the famous connection would help launch the two friends on their political careers.

Upon graduation from university, Milosevic held several Communist Party positions in the Belgrade city government. Stambolic, with the help of his powerful uncle, was fast headed up the ladder of national politics, and he brought his trusted best friend along with him every step of the way. In 1968 Milosevic began work at Technogas, Serbia's gas utility company, where Stambolic was already employed as an executive. By 1973, when Stambolic left for a more promising political position, he saw to it that his friend was made the company's director general. By 1978 Milosevic was appointed president of the largest state-run bank, Beobank. Stambolic was by then the prime minister of Serbia, one of the federal republics of what was then called the Socialist Federated Republic of Yugoslavia.

During this period, Milosevic took many trips to the United States, mastered the English language, and studied the American economic and political system. Years later, he would use this experience to dupe European and U.S. diplomats into believing that he was a modernizing liberal like Michail Gorbachev.

Still riding on Stambolic's coattails, in 1984 Milosevic was chosen to follow his friend as the Belgrade party chief, while Stambolic became the Communist Party leader of Serbia, one of the most powerful positions in the country. It was as Belgrade party boss that Milosevic acquired the reputation of a hardliner. He actively opposed all demands for liberalization or reform. A year later, as Stambolic was about to become president of Serbia, Milosevic's name was mentioned to succeed Stambolic as leader of the Serbian Communist Party. To pave the way for this appointment, Milosevic astutely cultivated the support of the media, in particular *Politika,* then Belgrade's leading newspaper. Milosevic avoided the traditional methods of punishing uncooperative journalists. Rather, he manipulated the media by gathering together a group of reporters who could easily be bribed.

In January of 1986 Stambolic became president of Serbia. Milosevic, in turn, was bestowed the position of Serbian Communist Party leader, against the desires of the liberals within the party who opposed Milosevic's nomination, including Mira's father, Moma Markovic, and her uncle, Draza Markovic. Stambolic had repeatedly rewarded his trusted friend Milosevic throughout his career. All Stambolic ever demanded in return was fealty. And all along, Milosevic never displayed anything but that. Stambolic had no idea that behind the scenes Mira Markovic was inciting her husband's political aspirations and eroding his loyalty. Mira helped Slobodan write his speeches, and together they began to gather support among the reactionaries and fundamentalists whom Stambolic had marginalized. Milosevic hid his political ambitions well. Stambolic, the godfather of Milosevic's children, the mentor, and the friend who told others that "I love him like a brother," never saw the ultimate betrayal coming.

The Grab for Power

In the autumn of 1986 the Serbian Academy of Arts and Sciences produced a memorandum consisting of inflammatory nationalistic propaganda. It was intended to be circulated only within the Serbian leadership but was leaked to the press. Its claims of collusion by Croatia and Slovenia against Serbia and the exploitation of Serbia's wealth by Tito, who had died in 1980, fueled an outpouring of Serb nationalist sentiment. Leaders in the other Yugoslav republics condemned the memorandum as evidence of Serbia's expansionist desires.

Under Tito's reign any talk of nationalism had been vilified. Tito knew that unchecked nationalism could easily lead to the division and destruction of Yugoslavia. As president of Serbia, Stambolic sought to walk a tightrope between the yearnings of the Serb intellectual community and his own desire to discourage ethnic nationalism, which he viewed as dangerous.

In the spring of 1987, Stambolic sent Milosevic to quell a group of Serbs from Kosovo who had been complaining about being mistreated by that region's ethnic Albanian majority. This meeting became the defining moment in Milosevic's political career. On his arrival he confronted fifteen thousand Kosovar Serbs. The local police, who were mostly ethnic Albanian, tried to control the unruly crowd. Rocks were thrown. The throng screamed that they were being beaten. Milosevic rose to the occasion. When he addressed the people, his message was one steeped in ethnic nationalism:

> No one has the right to beat our people! First of all my friends, I want to tell you that you must stay put. This is your land, these are your homes, these are your fields, your gardens, and your memories. You won't leave your land will you?
>
> Your lives are difficult because you are victims of oppression and injustice. The Serbian and Montenegrin spirit has never given in to hardship; it does not flee in battle, or flag in hard times.
>
> You must stay. Stay for your ancestors, stay for your children. Would you shame your ancestors and disappoint your children?
>
> There will be no tyranny on this soil. We will win this battle. Yugoslavia does not exist without Kosovo. Yugoslavia will disintegrate without Kosovo. Yugoslavia and Serbia will not give it away.

Milosevic arranged for a film of this speech to be repeatedly broadcast by a Belgrade television station run by a close friend of Mira's. Overnight, the speech transformed Milosevic into a Serb national hero. When he returned to Belgrade, he told officials that his extemporaneous remarks were the only available means to avoid bloodshed. He continued to denounce nationalism to the party leadership. It was revealed only much later that Milosevic and Mira had orchestrated the entire incident and that his words were well rehearsed.

Soon another spark would ignite the nationalistic fervor that was brewing beneath the surface of Serbian politics. A psychologically disturbed ethnic Albanian member of the Yugoslav National Army stormed into a barracks and killed six of his military comrades. While only one of the victims was a Serb, the attack was ascribed to the assassin's nationalistic motives. Speaking on behalf of Stambolic, the Belgrade party chief, Drasgia Pavlovic, called a press conference to warn of the dangers of anti-Albanian sentiments, intolerance, and nationalism to the stability of Yugoslavia. Milosevic saw this as the opportunity to make his ultimate power grab.

Behind the scenes, Milosevic and Markovic used Pavlovic as the wedge to divide the party leadership and seize control. Milosevic employed one of his loyal journalists to attack Pavlovic, setting the stage for the Belgrade party chief's ouster. The case against Pavlovic brought division to the party leadership, forcing each member to choose sides. The supporters of Pavlovic included many of the most senior Serbian Communist Party members, including Stambolic himself. But the majority of members were in favor of Pavlovic's dismissal. Though he knew that Milosevic was determined to bring down Pavlovic, Stambolic did not suspect that his most trusted friend would use the opportunity to force Stambolic's removal at the same time. However, on September 23, 1987, at the Eighth Plenary Session of the Communist Party, after a heated twenty-hour debate, Pavlovic was forced to resign. Milosevic then told his old friend, "I'm sorry, but your position has become untenable."

From then on, Milosevic, with the counsel of his wife, whipped Serbia into a nationalist frenzy that ultimately contributed to the disintegration of Yugoslavia and the economic and physical destruction of Serbia. Milosevic harnessed nationalist sentiment to establish his control over the Serb government, but his goal was merely to acquire the power of the top office. After suceeding Stambolic as president of Serbia in 1989, Milosevic again employed nationalist sentiment to wage war on the independence-minded Yugoslav republics, but his goal was merely to maintain the power he had seized. During this time, he was reelected president of Serbia twice and then in 1997 was elected president of the Federal Republic of Yugoslavia, consisting of Serbia and Montenegro. The Milosevic family grew exceedingly rich through their control of trade, finance, and every other aspect of business life. Those who supported Milosevic shared in the profits; those who opposed him faced jail and, in several cases, death. One of Milosevic's political opponents was gunned down in an underground garage; a second, in a pizzeria; a third, in a parking lot. In none of these cases were the murderers ever identified.

After losing four wars in eight years, Milosevic was finally driven from office in October 2000 in the face of a popular revolt, by a population that would no longer believe him and that would no longer sacrifice themselves for his causes. Those who knew Milosevic as a youth could never have predicted the narcissistic and brutal ruler he became. His ruthless quest for power, fueled by his wife's ambitions, were a surprise even to his closest friend, whose betrayal by him foreshadowed his betrayal of the Serb people.

CHAPTER 3

Key Events Leading to the Milosevic Prosecution

To understand the Milosevic trial, some understanding of the historical context that fomented the commission of horrific atrocities in the former Yugoslavia during the 1990s is essential. This chapter provides a time line of the major events leading to the Yugoslav crisis, the creation of the International Criminal Tribunal for the Former Yugoslavia (ICTY), and the trial of Slobodan Milosevic.

- **1389–1918**

    In 1389, Ottoman Turks defeat Serbian forces at the battle of Kosovo Polje, beginning a long period of Ottoman subjugation of the Balkans and sowing the seeds of the modern ethnic conflict.

    Ethnic conflict in the Balkans goes back nearly seven hundred years. Although the people of the different regions of the former Yugoslavia—Croatia, Serbia, Montenegro, Bosnia and Herzegovina—shared a common language (Serbo-Croatian) and physical characteristics (Slavic), differences in their religions and historical experiences led to the growth of strong separate ethnic identities.

    By the ninth century, Christianity had become the predominant faith throughout the region, with the western portion (what is

13

now Croatia and Slovenia) largely Roman Catholic and the eastern section (Bosnia and Herzegovina, Serbia, Montenegro, and Macedonia) mostly Eastern Orthodox. The defining moment in the early history of the region occurred on St. Vitus Day (June 28) in 1389, when the Ottoman Turks defeated Serbian forces at the battle of Kosovo Polje (Field of the Blackbirds). Thereafter, the eastern portions of the Balkans were plunged into a period of Ottoman occupation from which they did not emerge until the early twentieth century.

The Ottomans eventually advanced as far as the gates of Vienna before being repulsed. The western and northern borders of their European territories formed a boundary with predecessors of the Austro-Hungarian Empire. A military frontier on that boundary existed from the sixteenth century. This military frontier is said to account for much of the present-day Serb population in the area, people who had been encouraged to settle so as to provide a loyal population base and, potentially, a border defense force.

During the Ottoman subjugation, many of the Balkan peoples were able to preserve their culture by accepting second-class status within the Ottoman Empire. Others (predominantly in the cities of what is now Bosnia and Herzegovina) converted to Islam to avoid persecution and the oppressive taxes required of non-Muslims. Serbian hostility toward Bosnian Muslims today stems in part from what Serbs believe was a betrayal of the true faith by these Bosnians' ancestors over six hundred years ago and their alliance with the Ottoman occupiers. While Serbia, Montenegro, and Bosnia and Herzegovina existed under five centuries of Ottoman domination, the Catholic Slovenes and Croats were absorbed by the Hapsburg Empire and were influenced by centuries of close contact with Austria, Hungary, and Italy. The Croats have lived principally in the southwest, adjacent to the Dalmatian coast of the Adriatic Sea.

As the ICTY noted in its first major trial, each of the peoples in the region—Serbs, Croats, and Bosnian Muslims—had, in medieval times, its era of empire and greatness. "For Serbs the heroic but unsuccessful resistance of the Serb nation to Turkish invasion, culminating in their defeat in the battle of Kosovo, remains an emotional event, symbolic of Serb courage," said the Tribunal. "Nationalistic Serbs and Croats in particular each rely on long-past days of empire in support of their claims, necessarily conflicting, to a Greater Serbia and a Greater Croatia. For each, Bosnia and Herzegovina is of particular interest, containing as it does substantial Serb and Croat populations as well as an even larger Muslim population but having no single ethnic group as a majority of the population." Until 1878 Bosnia and Herzegovina remained under Ottoman rule. In that year the Austro-Hungarian Empire occupied Bosnia and Herzegovina and began to administer it.

• 1918–1941

Creation of the Kingdom of Serbs, Croats, and Slovenes under the crown of Peter I.

Two Balkan wars were fought in 1912 and 1913, resulting in the liberation of most of Balkan region from Ottoman control. On virtually all sides, the wars were characterized by terrible brutality, including terror and persecution of civilian populations. Having expelled the Turks, Serb nationalists turned their attention to the Hapsburg Empire, which had annexed Bosnia and Herzegovina in 1908. In one of the twentieth century's defining moments, Gavrilo Princip, a Bosnian Serb nationalist, assassinated Austrian Archduke Franz Ferdinand in Sarajevo on June 28, 1914. It was no coincidence that the archduke, who was heir to the Hapsburg throne, was killed on the anniversary of the battle of Kosovo. Mobilization of the great powers ensued, and soon, as Sir Edward Grey put it, the lights began going out around Europe. World War I had been set off by the Bosnian powder keg.

Balkan independence from foreign domination was finally realized after World War I. In a sense, it was the promise of self-determination from Woodrow Wilson's famous "Fourteen Points." The Hapsburg Empire was broken apart, and King Alexander of Serbia was authorized by the Great Powers to proclaim the Kingdom of Serbs, Croats, and Slovenes. In 1929 it became known as Yugoslavia, meaning "Land of the South Slavs." According to the ICTY,

> [T]he concept of a state of the south Slavs, who shared a common language and common ethnic origins, had evolved in the minds of Croatian intellectuals during the nineteenth century side by side with the growth amongst Serbs of the concept of a Greater Serbia. With the disintegration of the Ottoman and Austro-Hungarian Empires after World War I, these two disparate concepts, coupled with the status of Serbia as one of the allied powers, led to the creation of the postwar state of Yugoslavia. It was, however, an uneasy marriage of two ill-matched concepts and in the interwar years the nation experienced acute tensions of an ethno-national character.

The unity achieved under King Alexander was fragile, with the Croats pushing for ever greater self-government within a looser confederation. In 1929, supported by Italian dictator Benito Mussolini, the Ustasha (meaning "uprising") movement was born, committed to the goal of Croatian independence—if necessary, through violence. In 1934 a member of the Ustasha assassinated King Alexander, and a weak regency was appointed to rule in place of Alexander's ten-year-old son. This set the stage for the invasion of Yugoslavia by the Axis powers in 1941.

• 1941–1944

The Axis powers invade Yugoslavia and create the Ustasha independent state of Croatia, whose regime persecutes the Serbs.

During World War II, the Axis powers occupied Yugoslavia, partitioned the country into German and Italian spheres of influence, and transferred other areas to Bulgarian and Hungarian control. Croatia became a puppet state (comprised of today's Croatia and Bosnia and Herzegovina) of Hitler's Nazi Germany, with the Ustasha leader Ante Pavelic placed in charge. One minister in the Ustasha regime promised to kill a third of the Serbs in Croatia, deport another third by force, and convert the remaining third to Catholicism. Another minister urged that the puppet

Croatian state be cleansed of "Serbian dirt." The Ustasha established an extermination camp at Jasenovac that rivaled the infamous Nazi death camps at Auschwitz and elsewhere in its brutal efficiency. In all, over five hundred thousand Serbs were killed and a million were driven from the territory to seek refuge in other countries. At one point, the German authorities were reportedly forced to close the Danube to swimming because of the large number of Serb corpses being thrown into the river by the Croatian Ustasha.

• 1944–1980

Josip Broz Tito emerges as leader of Partisan resistance, which ultimately secures control over the territory of Yugoslavia.

Resistance to the Axis occupation of Yugoslavia came from the communist Partisan forces, who were predominantly Serb. Led by the Croatian-born Josip Broz Tito and supported by the Allies, the Partisans eventually secured control over the entire Yugoslav territory. In revenge for the Croatian atrocities, the Partisans executed over a hundred thousand Croatian prisoners when the Ustasha surrendered in May 1946.

After the war, Tito established a federal system in Yugoslavia consisting of six republics—Serbia, Croatia, Slovenia, Bosnia and Herzegovina, Macedonia, and Montenegro—and two autonomous provinces, Kosovo and Vojvodina, located within the Republic of Serbia. The reordered internal boundaries were aimed at containing Serbian nationalism by stranding Serb minorities in each of the republics outside Serbia itself. In addition, Tito successfully dealt with ethnic tensions within and among the republics. The constitution provided a range of checks and balances to ensure the coexistence of the various ethnic groups within the Yugoslav state. There was also stern repression at the hands of the secret police, known as the GZNA. As the ICTY has noted, "[t]he years from 1945 to 1990 had no tales of ethnic atrocities to tell. Marshal Tito and his communist regime took stern measures to suppress and keep suppressed all nationalist tendencies."

In 1948 Soviet premier Joseph Stalin expelled Yugoslavia from the Cominform, an organization of communist states, for "pursuing an unfriendly policy towards the Soviet Union." This action led to fears of a Soviet attack, a syndrome that intensified after the Soviet invasion of Czechoslovakia in 1968. As much as anything else, the Soviet threat provided the glue that held Tito's Yugoslavia together. Tito's death, on May 4, 1980, and the collapse of the Soviet threat in the late 1980's unleashed the long-festering centrifugal forces that would soon lead to Yugoslavia's disintegration.

- **1986**

The memorandum of the Serb Academy of Arts and Sciences is published, becoming the manifesto of the Serb nationalist movement and paving the way for Slobodan Milosevic's rise to power.

In 1986 members of the Serbian Academy of Arts and Sciences prepared a manifesto attacking the Yugoslav constitution. The document, known as the SAAS Memorandum, argued that Tito had consistently discriminated against the Serbs and that Serbia had been subject to economic domination by Croatia and Slovenia.

Later that year Slobodan Milosevic, riding a wave of Serbian nationalism, became Serbian Communist Party chief. Milosevic solidified his position by provoking and then using federal troops to ruthlessly crush successive crises in the Serb province of Kosovo, where ethnic Albanians outnumbered Serbs by about ten to one. Kosovo became Milosevic's launching pad in his quest to extend his power to the rest of Yugoslavia.

- **1990**

Hard-line leaders assume power in the Yugoslav republics.

The ascent of Milosevic's hard-line nationalist government in Serbia fanned anti-Serb nationalism in the republics of Croatia and Slovenia. At the same time, Milosevic's efforts to create a more centralized Yugoslavia under Serbian dominance engendered strident resistance from the leaders of Croatia and Slovenia, Franjo Tudjman and Milan Kucan respectively. The Croat and Slovene leaders sought to convert Yugoslavia into a loose confederation where Serbian influence would be diluted.

- **1991**

SPRING

Milosevic provokes a constitutional crisis, prompting Slovenia and Croatia to declare their independence from Yugoslavia.

Flexing his political muscle, in the spring of 1991 Milosevic blocked Stipe Mesic, a Croat, from assuming the federal presidency, despite the fact that the Yugoslav constitution provided that the presidency was to rotate annually among the republics and it was Croatia's turn to fill the office. A series of negotiations with Milosevic over a new Yugoslav constitution proved futile. On June 25, 1991, Croatia and Slovenia declared their independence, but without offering concrete guarantees for the security of the five hundred thousand Serbs living within their borders. The European Community (predecessor of the European Union) was able to negotiate an agreement whereby Croatia agreed to wait three months before making its declaration of independence effective.

LATE JUNE

The Yugoslav army invades Slovenia and Croatia.

A few days before Croatia and Slovenia's declarations of independence, U.S. Secretary of State James Baker, visiting Belgrade, had warned of the "dangers of disintegration," and urged that Yugoslavia maintain "territorial integrity." He added that the United States "would not recognize unilateral declarations of independence." Milosevic took this as a green light to use force to halt secession and to protect the Serbs living in Croatia and

Slovenia. He began by sending the Serb-dominated Yugoslav National Army (JNA) into Slovenia to crush that republic's nascent militia. After the Slovenes withstood repeated attacks and actually defeated the JNA in several engagements, Milosevic agreed to a European Community–brokered cease-fire. Then he turned his attention to Croatia.

The JNA, aided by local Serbian insurgents, inflicted heavy casualties on the inexperienced and outgunned Croatian forces and quickly took control of one-third of Croatia's territory. On November 20, 1991, one of the Yugoslav conflict's most egregious acts was committed when Serb forces captured the Croatian town of Vukovar after an appalling siege. Upon entering the city, Serb forces massacred some two hundred Croatian patients (mostly wounded soldiers) of the Vukovar hospital, disposing of their bodies in a mass grave that was later discovered by United Nations forensic investigators. JNA forces also launched an attack on the Croatian town of Dubrovnik, located at the southern tip of the Dalmatian coast. A world heritage site protected by the UN Education, Scientific, and Cultural Organization (UNESCO), Dubrovnik was shelled mercilessly at great cost to the town's population, not to mention the loss to posterity of irreplaceable monuments.

SEPTEMBER

The United Nations Security Council, at the request of the Yugoslav government in Belgrade, adopts Resolution 713, imposing an arms embargo on the territory of Yugoslavia.

A few months after fighting broke out in Slovenia and Croatia in 1991, Belgrade requested that the Security Council impose an arms embargo on Yugoslavia to prevent an escalation of the conflict. Later the Security Council reaffirmed that its arms embargo would continue to apply to all parts of the former Yugoslavia, "any decisions on the question of the recognition of the independence of certain republics notwithstanding." The only state truly affected by the arms embargo was Bosnia and Herzegovina, which was left with no means to defend itself, while Serbia had all the military equipment and supplies it needed.

- **1992**

JANUARY

United Nations envoy Cyrus Vance negotiates a cease-fire between Croatian and Serbian forces in Croatia, which agree to the deployment of United Nations peacekeepers in the Serb-held territories.

For six months, repeated efforts by the European Community and the Conference on Security and Cooperation in Europe (CSCE, the forerunner of the Organization for Security and Cooperation in Europe, or OSCE) to broker a durable cease-fire in Croatia failed to yield tangible success. Finally, in January of 1992, after thousands had been killed in the fighting, Croatia and Serbia agreed to the deployment of a United Nations peace-keeping force (known as UNPROFOR) to oversee the withdrawal of the JNA and the disarming of local forces in the areas of conflict inside Croatia. Croatia obtained international recognition, first from Germany, then from other members of the European Community and the United States. During the next four years, under cover of the United Nations and backed by Germany and the United States, Croatia would arm and make preparations for a successful campaign to retake territory it had lost at the time of the cease-fire.

MARCH–APRIL

Bosnia declares its independence from Yugoslavia, prompting the outbreak of war between the Bosnian government and Bosnian Serb paramilitary troops aided by JNA forces.

With the events in Croatia as a backdrop, Bosnian Muslims were forced to choose between remaining in what was becoming a Serbian ethnic dictatorship or seeking a hazardous independence. The leader of the Bosnian Serb political party, SDS (Srpska demokratska stranka Bosne i Hercegovine, or Serbian Democratic Party of Bosnia and Herzegovina), Radovan Karadzic, warned that pursuing independence would "make the Muslim people disappear, because the Muslims cannot defend themselves if there is war." But his threatening words were not heeded. On March 1, 1992, the Muslim and Croatian people of Bosnia and Herzegovina voted overwhelmingly for independence. At the time of the vote, Bosnia consisted of three main ethnic groups: Muslims (44 percent of the population), Serbs (31 percent), and Croats (17 percent).* While these groups are defined on the basis of religion, Bosnia was largely a secular society. A 1985 survey found that only 17 percent of its people considered themselves believers and interfaith marriage was extremely common.

On April 6 the European Community recognized the new independent nation of Bosnia and Herzegovina and the United States followed suit the next day. That same day, the Bosnian Serbs, under the leadership of their self-styled president, Radovan Karadzic, proclaimed the formation of an independent "Republika Srpska" (Serbian Republic of Bosnia and Herzegovina), whose government was located in the city of Pale in southeastern Bosnia, not far from Sarajevo.

The Serbs immediately launched attacks against the Croatian and Muslim populations in northeastern and southern Bosnia with the goal of connecting Serb-populated regions in northern and western Bosnia to Serbia in the east. Assisted by some forty-five thousand JNA troops the Serb insurgent forces seized control, municipality by municipality, of 70 percent of Bosnia's territory. By the middle of April, the Muslims were left with control of only a few islands of territory within Bosnia—Sarajevo, Mostar, Bihac, Tusla, Srebrenica, and Gorazde. These enclaves were shelled relentlessly by JNA and Serb insurgent forces in the years to follow.

MAY

The Federal Republic of Yugoslavia (Serbia-Montenegro) demobilizes JNA forces in Bosnia, leaving behind heavy weapons and thousands of troops to form a new Serb paramilitary force.

---

* According to the International Criminal Tribunal for the former Yugoslavia, in one of its earliest judgments, "Since all three population groups are Slav it is, no doubt, inaccurate to speak of three different ethnic groups; however, this appears to be accepted common usage."

On May 19, 1992, in an unsuccessful attempt to head off the threat of United Nations sanctions against Serbia for its involvement in the hostilities in Bosnia, Serbia announced the withdrawal of the JNA from Bosnia and Herzegovina. When the JNA pulled out, however, it left behind 85 percent of the "demobilized" officers and men, as well as most of the army's equipment. The demobilized troops, under the command of former JNA 9th Army Corps chief of staff, Ratko Mladic, together with local insurgents and Serbia-based militias, became a new Bosnian Serb army. This new army, however, continued to receive assistance and instructions from Serbia. Not deceived by this tactic, on May 30 the UN Security Council adopted Resolution 757, which imposed a sweeping trade embargo on Serbia and Montenegro.

However, the initial draft of the Security Council sanctions resolution was substantially watered down to satisfy Russian objections. For example, an exception was inserted into the resolution allowing for the transshipment of goods across the territory of Serbia. These goods were readily diverted to destinations within Serbia itself. Another exception allowed for the shipment of humanitarian items to Serbia, including cigarettes, vodka, clothing, and heating oil, which were freely diverted to the Serb army and paramilitary forces. The embargo, moreover, did not cover shipments to Serb-controlled territories in Bosnia. Nor did the resolution provide for effective enforcement measures such as maritime interdiction of vessels trading with Serbia-Montenegro or placement of monitors at Serbia's borders. Thus, Serbia easily succeeded in circumventing the sanctions. Even after the sanctions were incrementally strengthened through the adoption of Resolution 787 in November 1992 and Resolution 820 in April 1993, the Security Council's measures had no perceptible impact on the willingness or ability of the Bosnian Serbs to continue to wage war and to commit atrocities.

AUGUST–OCTOBER

Britain's Independent Television News (ITN) broadcasts a film of emaciated detainees at the Omarska camp, prompting the UN Security Council to establish the United Nations

Commission of Experts to investigate alleged atrocities in the Balkans.

On August 6, 1992, Penny Marshall of Independent Television News (ITN) filmed conditions at the notorious Omarska concentration camp, which was run by the Serbs in northern Bosnia. She captured startling footage: "Muslim men at various stages of human decay and affliction; the bones of their elbows and wrists protrude like pieces of jagged stone from the pencil thin stalks to which their arms have been reduced." The ITN footage ignited an international outcry for something to be done to stop the atrocities.

The day after the ITN footage of Omarska aired worldwide, U.S. president George Bush told a news conference, "We know there is horror in these detention camps. But in all honesty, I can't confirm to you some of the claims that there is indeed a genocidal process going on there." Thereafter, U.S. officials were instructed to avoid using the "genocide" label with respect to Bosnia so as not to trigger obligations under the 1948 Genocide Convention, which imposes a duty to prevent and punish acts of genocide. In response, for the first time since the Vietnam war, a series of State Department officials resigned in protest at the administration's policy of nonintervention.

In the face of growing public pressure to respond to the Bosnian atrocities, on August 13, 1992, the Security Council adopted Resolution 771, calling upon states and international humanitarian organizations to submit to the council "substantiated information" in their possession concerning war crimes in the former Yugoslavia. Two months later, on October 6, 1992, the Security Council adopted Resolution 780, establishing an impartial Commission of Experts to assess the information submitted pursuant to Resolution 771, as well as information obtained through the commission's own investigations or efforts.

DECEMBER

U.S. secretary of state Lawrence Eagleburger delivers his "naming names" speech.

At a session of Yugoslav peace talks that were held in Geneva in December 1992, sponsored by the United Nations and the European Union, the U.S. Secretary of State Lawrence Eagleburger dropped a bombshell by announcing that his government had identified ten suspected war criminals who it thought should be brought to trial before a modern-day Nuremberg Tribunal. This has become known in U.S. government circles as the "naming names" speech. The list of persons named by Eagleburger included Radovan Karadzic, the political leader of the Bosnian Serbs; General Ratko Mladic, the Bosnian Serbs' military leader; and Slobodan Milosevic, president of the Federal Republic of Yugoslavia (Serbia and Montenegro). Eagleburger told the press that the "naming names" speech had been prompted by his recent meeting with Elie Wiesel, the noted author and survivor of Nazi death camps. "He persuaded me," Eagleburger said, "that these people needed to be named and that this conduct could not go on."

- **1993**

FEBRUARY

The United Nations War Crimes Commission issues its preliminary report, prompting the Security Council to adopt Resolution 808, deciding to establish a War Crimes Tribunal.

In early February of 1993 the Commission of Experts submitted its preliminary report to the Security Council. The report concluded that war crimes, crimes against humanity, and genocide had been committed in Bosnia and recommended the creation of an international criminal tribunal to prosecute the perpetrators. A few weeks later, on February 22, 1993, the Security Council adopted Resolution 808, in which it decided in principle to establish an international tribunal "for the prosecution of persons responsible for serious violations of international humanitarian law committed in the territory of the former Yugoslavia since 1991."

None of the permanent members of the Security Council, however, apparently expected such a tribunal to actually prosecute the Serb and Bosnian Serb leaders. Instead, they reportedly saw the Tribunal's creation as an instrument for pacifying critics. It would generate the appearance of action against gross violations of human rights, but without great sacrifice of blood or money. In addition to the public relations benefit, they recognized that, even without bringing a single perpetrator to trial, an international indictment and arrest warrant could serve to isolate offending leaders diplomatically, strengthen the hand of domestic rivals, and fortify the international political will to expand economic sanctions or approve air strikes.

MARCH

The Security Council adopts Resolution 816, authorizing enforcement of the "no-fly zone" over Bosnia through NATO air strikes in close coordination with the United Nations secretary-general.

Bosnian Serb aircraft were attacking civilian targets from their air base in the Bosnian Serb–controlled city of Banja Luka. Bosnian Muslims, who had no air force, were extremely vulnerable to such "ethnic cleansing by air" and their casualties quickly mounted. In response, on October 9, 1992, the Security Council adopted Resolution 781, imposing a "no-fly zone" over Bosnia. At the urging of the British and French, the clause providing for enforcement of the no-fly zone was omitted from the resolution. Instead, the resolution called only for monitors to report on violations. They had plenty to report. During the next six months there were over 465 documented violations of the no-fly zone. Yet it was not until March 31, 1993, that the Security Council adopted Resolution 816, authorizing the North Atlantic Treaty Organization to enforce the no-fly zone. Only on February 8, 1994, did NATO actually begin shooting down Serb aircraft violating the ban.

APRIL

The Security Council adopts resolutions designating six Muslim enclaves as "safe areas."

In the spring of 1993, the Serbs began to attack the final Muslim enclaves in Bosnia and Herzegovina: Srebrenica, Sarajevo, Tuzla,

Zepa, Gorazde, and Bihac. The Security Council responded by adopting Resolutions 819 and 824, declaring these to be "safe areas," off-limits to armed attack. As a *quid pro quo* for the withdrawal of Serb forces, the UN peacekeeping force, UNPROFOR, was assigned the task of overseeing the demilitarization of the safe areas. Yet the Security Council provided no real enforcement component to the safe area concept. While the UNPROFOR commander indicated that it would take 35,000 troops to protect the safe areas, the council irresponsibly chose the "light option" of a 7,500 troop reinforcement to carry out the mandate.

MAY

The Security Council adopts Resolution 827, establishing the International Criminal Tribunal for the Former Yugoslavia (ICTY).

On May 25, 1993, the Security Council, acting under Chapter VII of the Charter of the United Nations, unanimously adopted the Statute of the International Tribunal for the Prosecution of Persons Responsible for Serious Violations of International Humanitarian Law Committed in the Territory of the Former Yugoslavia since 1991. The statute of the ICTY had been drafted by the UN Office of Legal Affairs. The Tribunal was given jurisdiction over four different international crimes committed in the territory of the former Yugoslavia after January 1, 1991: grave breaches of the Geneva Conventions of August 12, 1949, violations of the laws or customs of war, genocide, and crimes against humanity. The Tribunal was not, however, given a constabulary or any other means to enforce its arrest orders, though Member states of the United Nations were ordered by the Security Council to cooperate fully with the Tribunal.

SEPTEMBER

The United Nations General Assembly elects the Tribunal's judges.

In ten contentious rounds of voting, the UN General Assembly elected the Yugoslavia Tribunal's eleven judges. The nine men and two women elected were from both civil and common law countries. Three were from Asia, two from Europe, two from Africa, two from North America, and one each from Latin America and Australia. The nominee from Russia, however, was defeated in the election, apparently to avoid a pro-Serb bias. Among those elected was an American, Gabrielle Kirk McDonald, a former federal district judge and law professor who presided over the Tribunal's first prosecution and later became the Tribunal's president.

The judges soon began drafting the rules of procedure and evidence. These would fill many of the gaps in the relatively laconic statute. They had to craft an original, hybrid tribunal, drawing upon procedural and evidentiary principles of a variety of different legal systems. Much compromise was required as the judges learned how justice was done in other parts of the world. But the judges could not begin their real work until individual suspects had actually been arrested and charged. And that required appointment of a prosecutor. Without an effective prosecutor, the Tribunal simply could not function.

• 1994

FEBRUARY

Serbs fire a mortar bomb into the open-air market in the center of Sarajevo, killing forty-nine civilians and wounding two hundred others.

JULY

The United Nations Security Council appoints Richard Goldstone to be the Tribunal's first prosecutor.

After a series of nominees had been vetoed by various members of the Security Council, on July 7, 1994, the council approved the appointment of Richard Goldstone to be the Tribunal's first prosecutor (an initial appointee never really took office, and resigned within a few months). Goldstone was a distinguished South African judge with impeccable credentials in the struggle against *apartheid*. Goldstone had presided over a commission that investigated crimes under South Africa's former racist regime. Only a few weeks before being chosen as the prosecutor of the ICTY, he had been appointed to the country's new Constitutional Court. Nelson Mandela himself reluctantly agreed to give Goldstone a two-year leave from his important functions in South Africa.

Late in 1994, the Office of the prosecutor learned of a Serb militiaman who had been spotted working in a Munich café and arrested by German authorities. Proceedings by German courts against Dusko Tadic had already begun when the ICTY prosecutor requested the suspect be transferred to The Hague to stand trial. The Tribunal had a customer; it was in business. But Tadic was a small-time player, and his crimes, while horrendous, could hardly be distinguished from those of thousands like him on all sides of the conflict. Even in 1995, it was clear enough that the Tribunal had been created to fry bigger fish than Dusko Tadic.

- **1995**

JULY

Bosnian Serb forces launch an attack on the United Nations safe areas.

When the Serbs began attacking the safe areas, the United Nations Peacekeeping forces that had been assigned to provide security retreated. Tens of thousands of defenseless civilians were massacred and carted off to mass graves in the nearby countryside. Srebrenica, in eastern Bosnia, was the scene of a particularly horrible atrocity. Some seven thousand unarmed men and boys were lined up alongside trenches and summarily executed with machine guns. "Historians will show," wrote the editors of *The New Republic* shortly after the Srebrenica massacre, "that the most important allies of the Bosnian Serbs have been the peacekeeping forces of the United Nations."

Radovan Karadzic and Ratko Mladic are indicted by the International Criminal Tribunal for the Former Yugoslavia.

On July 24, 1995, Radovan Karadzic, the leader of the Bosnian Serbs, and Ratko Mladic, the commander of the Bosnian Serb army, were indicted by the Yugoslavia war crimes tribunal for grave breaches of the Geneva Convention, violations of the laws and customs of war, genocide, and crimes against humanity committed in Bosnia. According to the indictment, "Bosnian Muslim and Bosnian Croat civilians were persecuted on national, political and religious grounds throughout the Republic of Bosnia and Herzegovina. Thousands of them were interned in detention facilities where they were subjected to widespread acts of physical and psychological abuse and to inhumane conditions." The two were also charged with targeting political leaders, intellectuals, and professionals; sponsoring campaigns of rape and sexual violence; deportating and shelling civilian gatherings; and plundering and destroying property, including sacred sites. But of course, they remained at large.

AUGUST

Bosnian Serbs shell the Sarajevo marketplace again, prompting NATO to launch "Operation Deliberate Force."

A second Bosnian Serb mortar attack on the Sarajevo marketplace, on August 28, killed thirty-seven Muslim civilians. It prompted a reluctant NATO to finally approve a U.S. proposal for air strikes. Thus in August 1995 the United States launched "Operation Deliberate Force," a massive bombing campaign against Serb targets the purpose of which was to silence the Serb artillery and produce a diplomatic breakthrough. The stage was set for the negotiation of the Dayton Peace Accord.

NOVEMBER

Peace talks in Dayton, Ohio, produce the Dayton Peace Accord.

In November of 1995 the parties to the Yugoslav conflict and representatives of states with a special interest in the region known as the "Contact Group" (the United States, Russia, France, the United Kingdom, and Germany) gathered in Dayton, Ohio, to negotiate a series of accords designed to bring about an end to the war and the peaceful reintegration of Bosnia. The basic deal underlying the Dayton Accord was known as the "51-49" plan. The Bosnian-Croat federation would receive 51 percent of Bosnia, while the Bosnian Serbs would be entitled to 49 percent. While the two entities would have substantial autonomy, national policies would be set by a three-person presidency consisting of a Muslim, a Croat, and a Serb. Following the successful conclusion of the Dayton negotiations, the Security Council adopted Resolution 1031, authorizing the deployment of a NATO force in Bosnia, to be known as IFOR, to implement the accord.

Slobodan Milosevic was one of the signatories of the Dayton Accord. Indeed, he also took the place of the Bosnian Serbs' leaders, Karadzic and Mladic, who had been effectively marginalized as a result of their indictment by the ICTY the previous July. The Dayton Accord provided that "each Party shall comply with any order or request of the International Tribunal for the Former Yugoslavia for the arrest, detention, surrender of or access to persons who would otherwise be released and transferred under this Article, but who are accused of violations within the jurisdiction of the Tribunal. Each Party must detain persons reasonably suspected of such violations for a period of time sufficient to permit appropriate consultation with Tribunal authorities." Moreover, the accord stipulated that no one who was under indictment by the ICTY and who had failed to comply with one of its orders could stand for election in Bosnia and Herzegovina.

• 1996–1997

The Security Council lifts sanctions against the Bosnian Serb entity and the Federal Republic of Yugoslavia (Serbia-Montenegro), despite their refusal to cooperate with the Yugoslav Tribunal.

Following the signing of the Dayton Accord, on November 21, 1995, the Security Council adopted Resolution 1022, whereby it "suspend[ed] indefinitely with immediate effect" the economic sanctions that it had imposed against the Federal Republic of Yugoslavia and the Republika Srpska beginning in 1992. Resolution 1022 contained a potentially important provision for the reintroduction of economic sanctions in the event of non-compliance with the Dayton Accord requirement that the parties cooperate with the ICTY. However, that provision was never invoked, even when the Tribunal informed the Security Council that the Federal Republic of Yugoslavia and the Republika Srpska had refused to comply with the Tribunal's arrest warrants and that a number of persons indicted by the Tribunal continued to hold government positions in the Bosnian Serb territory. On October 1, 1996, the Security Council adopted Resolution 1074, terminating the Yugoslav sanctions once and for all, thus giving away a potentially effective mechanism for pressuring the Serbs to surrender indicted persons to the ICTY.

NATO forces decline to arrest Radovan Karadzic or Ratko Mladic in the forces' area of operation.

Despite the deployment of sixty thousand NATO troops in Bosnia in 1995 as part of the Dayton Accord and Security Council resolutions giving these troops the authority to arrest indicted war criminals, NATO troops declined to arrest indicted Bosnian Serb leader Radovan Karadzic when he passed through NATO checkpoints on several occasions in 1996. In August 1997, when NATO inspectors learned that indicted Bosnian Serb general Ratko Mladic was inside a bunker they had planned to inspect, they rescheduled their visit rather than confront the indicted war criminal.

According to the *Washington Post,* in the summer of 1997 the United States was forced at the last minute to abort plans for the apprehension of Radovan Karadzic when it was discovered that a senior French military officer had held secret meetings with Karadzic. Afterwards, senior Clinton administration officials acknowledged that "they were quite close to carrying it out, having determined how to arrange the capture and which troops would be involved." But after this incident no further attempt was made to apprehend the most wanted Bosnian Serb leaders,

Radovan Karadzic and Ratko Mladic. They still remained at large when the Milosevic trial got underway in February 2002.

Under the Dayton Agreement, Karadzic may have been forced to relinquish his official position, but like an evil puppet master, he retained effective power in the Republika Srpska to the detriment of a Bosnian peace. From behind the scenes Karadzic still runs the Serb nationalist–based party known as the SDS, which still controls the Republika Srpska's police, court system, media, and major industries in forty-nine of the country's sixty-one munici-palities. He also dominates a network of underground Bosnian Serb paramilitary organizations, whose plans include destabiliz-ing the peace process, creating opposition within the Bosnian Serb population in Republika Srpska, to the NATO troops and international agencies stirring up general animosity toward the Bosnian-Croat federation, and destroying any moderate Serb elements.

• 1998

Serb forces commit atrocities against ethnic Albanians in the Serb province of Kosovo.

With a fragile peace in Bosnia and Herzegovina, the crisis in the former Yugoslavia seemed only to shift focus to Kosovo, a province within the Republic of Serbia. Kosovo, whose popula-tion was predominantly of Albanian ethnicity and language, had enjoyed a large degree of autonomy under Tito, but this was taken away in the late 1980s with the rise of Serb nationalism. An armed organization emerged among the Kosovo Albanians known as the KLA (Kosovo Liberation Army or *Ushtria Çlirimtare e Kosovës*). In 1996 the KLA began attacking Serbian authorities, who responded with a brutal crackdown. It became increasingly apparent that another agenda was at work, namely the ethnic cleansing of large swaths of Kosovo so as to strengthen the position of the province's Serb minority. As part of their campaign, Serb police, army, and militias terrorized local civilian populations, murdered noncombatants, and laid siege to villages.

- **1999**

FEBRUARY

The government of Yugoslavia refuses to sign the peace agreement negotiated at Rambouillet, France.

Shortly after January 15, 1999, when Serb military forces massacred over forty civilians in the Kosovo town of Racak, the contact group (the United States, France, the United Kingdom, Germany, and Russia) mediated two rounds of peace negotiations in Rambouillet, France, between the government of the Federal Republic of Yugoslavia and the Kosovo Albanian leadership. A draft agreement provided for the withdrawal of Serb forces from Kosovo, the disarmament of the KLA, the establishment of an international peacekeeping force in Kosovo, and the creation of a process for determining Kosovo's final status after the expiry of a three-year period. At the end of the talks, the Kosovo delegation signed the agreement, but the Serb delegation refused. Instead, the Serbs continued their military campaign in Kosovo.

MARCH

NATO conducts a seventy-eight-day bombing campaign against the Federal Republic of Yugoslavia.

From March 24, 1999, through June 9, 1999, NATO conducted a seventy-eight-day bombing campaign against the Federal Republic of Yugoslavia. Although it had no authorization from the UN Security Council, NATO justified its action on grounds of morality (to stop atrocities in Kosovo) and security (to prevent the Kosovo conflict from spilling over to neighboring European countries). Russia and China criticized the NATO intervention. The Federal Republic of Yugoslavia filed an application before the International Court of Justice charging NATO powers with breaching the Charter of the United Nations.

MAY

The Yugoslavia Tribunal indicts Slobodan Milosevic for crimes against humanity in Kosovo.

On May 24, 1999, in the midst of the NATO bombing campaign, Slobodan Milosevic, president of the Federal Republic of Yugoslavia, along with four other high-ranking Yugoslav officials, was indicted for war crimes and crimes against humanity committed against the ethnic Albanians in Kosovo. Notably absent from the indictment is a charge of genocide—the most serious crime within the Tribunal's jurisdiction. Also conspicuously missing from the indictment are any charges relating to atrocities in Bosnia and Herzegovina, where from 1992 to 1995 Bosnian Serbs with the aid of the Yugoslav National Army reportedly killed 250,000 Muslims and "ethnically cleansed" two million others from Serb-controlled areas.

JUNE

Milosevic agrees to a peace accord, placing Kosovo under international administration.

With the threat of continuing NATO bombing, Slobodan Milosevic finally agreed to remove Serb military forces from Kosovo and allow the deployment of NATO forces and the creation of an interim administration operated by the United Nations. To formalize the arrangement, the UN Security Council adopted Resolution 1244, which established the mandate for the NATO deployment and set forth a framework for UN administration of Kosovo for an interim period.

• 2000

JUNE

The International Tribunal issues its report on alleged NATO war crimes, finding that no further investigation is warranted.

Shortly after the NATO air campaign concluded, several human rights organizations and lawyers' groups submitted reports to the Office of the prosecutor of the ICTY, alleging that NATO had committed war crimes within the Tribunal's jurisdiction. In an effort to demonstrate independence and evenhandedness, the Tribunal's prosecutor, Louise Arbour, ordered a preliminary review of the evidence and applicable law by an internal committee led by her chief legal adviser, William Fenrick, a former Canadian military lawyer. A year later, on June 8, 2000, the Tribunal's new prosecutor, Carla Del Ponte, publicly issued the report of the committee's findings. She decided that the evidence and accusations were not sufficient to justify any further investigation.

OCTOBER

Slobodan Milosevic resigns the presidency of the Federal Republic of Yugoslavia in the face of a mass popular revolt.

In the aftermath of the 1999 NATO bombing campaign, Milosevic's local popularity dropped to just 20 percent, the lowest approval rating in his thirteen-year rule. Serbia's economic woes, brought on by years of international sanctions and exacerbated by the damage NATO bombs had wrought, ultimately led to Milosevic's landslide defeat in the Yugoslav presidential election of September 2000. When the "official tally" nevertheless ruled Milosevic the winner, millions of Serbs took to the streets in protest.

As the throngs of protestors steadily grew outside government offices in Belgrade, there was fear around the world that Milosevic would quell the popular uprising by employing deadly force, as the Chinese had done in Tiananmen square. But rather than attack the protestors, the members of the local Serb army garrison joined them as they stormed various government buildings. Realizing that Milosevic's fate was now sealed, his confederates quickly scrambled for political cover. A few hours later, the Constitutional Court of Yugoslavia ruled that Milosevic's opponent, Vojislav Kostunica, had in fact captured over 50 percent of the vote. This was followed by the Serbian parliament's recognition of Kostunica's election as president. On October 6, 2000, Milosevic submitted his resignation.

- **2001**

APRIL

The new government of Yugoslavia arrests Milosevic for domestic prosecution.

In April 2001 the Kostunica government arrested Milosevic on charges of corruption, political assassination, and election fraud. To reward Kostunica for this action, the newly elected Bush administration provided Serbia with $50 million in foreign aid. The Bush foreign policy team felt that a Serb domestic prosecution would discredit Milosevic, possibly paving the way for his eventual trial before the International Criminal Tribunal. And even if Milosevic never made it to The Hague, at least he would rot in a Serb prison.

JUNE

The Yugoslav government transfers Milosevic to The Hague for trial.

While the Bush administration was content to see Milosevic tried in Serbia, the U.S. Senate Finance Committee chairman, Mitch McConnel, unilaterally inserted into the appropriations act a provision requiring Milosevic's surrender to The Hague as a precondition for the provision of any additional aid funds to Serbia. Even with billions of dollars in aid at stake, however, Vojislav Kostunica, backed up by a Yugoslav federal court ruling, refused to permit the extradition of Milosevic to The Hague. But in a move that caught everyone off guard, Kostunica's political rival, Prime Minister Zoran Djindjic, instructed the Serb police under his command to secretly take Milosevic to an American air base in Tuzla, Bosnia, from which Milosevic was transferred by military jet to The Hague on June 28, 2001.

In announcing the action, Djindjic said that he had been forced to take a "difficult but morally correct" decision to protect the interests of Serbia. Immediately thereafter, a furious Kostunica protested that the extradition of Milosevic was "illegal and unconstitutional." Other members of the Kostinica cabinet resigned in dissent, throwing the fragile Belgrade government into turmoil. But the political crisis quickly faded when, two days later, Yugoslavia was awarded $1.28 billion in aid by the United States and its European allies.

OCTOBER

ICTY indicts Milosevic on additional charges.

In October 2001 the International Criminal Tribunal issued an additional indictment against Milosevic, charging him with responsibility for war crimes and crimes against humanity in Croatia during late 1991. The prosecutor announced that yet another indictment was in preparation and that it would charge the crime of crimes, genocide. True to her word, a month later she obtained an indictment against Milosevic for genocide and other offenses committed in Bosnia and Herzegovina between 1992 and 1995.

In the meantime, Milosevic had appeared several times before the Tribunal in pretrial proceedings. Defiant and uncooperative, he refused to designate counsel and insisted on acting in his own defense. He charged that the Tribunal was biased and that it had been illegally constituted. The judges then appointed three distinguished defense lawyers as friends of the court, or *amici curiae*. They filed a preliminary motion raising the same arguments that Milosevic had invoked. In November the motion was dismissed by the three judges designated to hear the case.

The three judges also dismissed a motion from the prosecutor, who sought joinder of the three indictments. Her objective was to hold one big trial, rather than three separate proceedings. The trial judges' refusal to go along was appealed to the Appeals Chamber. In January 2002 the Appeals Chamber ordered the three cases joined.

• 2002

The Trial of Slobodan Milosevic begins on February 12, 2002.

CHAPTER 4

From Nuremberg to The Hague: The History of International Prosecution

The history of international war crimes trials begins with the 1474 prosecution of Peter von Hagenbach, a Burgundian governor. After it was discovered that his troops had raped and killed innocent civilians and pillaged their property during the occupation of Breisach, Germany, Hagenbach was tried before a tribunal of twenty-eight judges from the allied states of the Holy Roman Empire, which at that time included Austria, Bohemia, Luxembourg, Milan, the Netherlands, and Switzerland. Hagenbach was found guilty of murder, rape, and other crimes against the "laws of God and man," stripped of his knighthood, and sentenced to death.

It would be nearly five hundred years, however, before states would again join together to conduct an international war crimes trial. As World War I drew to a close, the Allied Powers established a commission to document war crimes committed by German troops. The Versailles Treaty, adopted in Paris in 1919, provided for war crimes prosecutions as well as an international trial of the German emperor, Kaiser Wilhelm II. But the provisions were never properly implemented. Instead, the Kaiser was given sanctuary in the Netherlands, then a neutral country. The Allied Powers consented to the trial of accused Germans before the German Supreme Court sitting at Leipzig. Of the 896 Germans accused of war crimes by the Allied Powers, only 12 were ever tried. Of these, 6 were convicted and given token sentences. The Turks fared even better. The Treaty of Sèvres also contemplated war crimes trials, but it never came into force. It was eventually replaced by the Treaty of Lausanne, which accorded an amnesty.

Despite the inadequacies of international justice following World War I, the idea of trials again became popular during World War II, leading ultimately to the establishment of the Nuremberg Tribunal. The events that prompted the Nuremberg Tribunal's formation in 1945 are probably more familiar to most than those that led to the creation of the International Criminal Tribunal for the former Yugoslavia a half-century later. Between 1933 and 1940 the Nazi regime established concentration camps where Jews, Communists, and opponents of the regime were incarcerated without trial. It progressively prohibited Jews from engaging in employment and participating in various areas of public life, stripped them of citizenship, and made marriage or sexual intimacy between Jews and German citizens a criminal offense. The Nazi regime forcibly annexed Austria and Czechoslovakia; invaded and occupied Poland, Denmark, Norway, Luxembourg, Holland, Belgium, and France; and then set in motion "the final solution to the Jewish problem" by establishing death camps at such places as Auschwitz, Treblinka, and Belzec where millions of Jews were exterminated.

Creation of the Nuremberg Tribunal

As Allied forces pressed into Germany and an end to the fighting in Europe came into sight, the Allies faced the challenge of deciding what to do with the surviving Nazi leaders who were responsible for these atrocities. Holding an international trial, however, was not their first preference. The British government opposed trying the Nazi leaders on the ground that their "guilt was so black" that it was "beyond the scope of judicial process." British prime minister Winston Churchill proposed the summary execution of the Nazi leaders. Soviet leader Joseph Stalin, however, urged that Nazi leaders be tried, much as he had done with dissidents in his own country during the purges of the 1930s. U.S. president Franklin D. Roosevelt initially appeared willing to go along with Churchill's proposal. But upon Roosevelt's death in April 1945, President Harry Truman made it clear that he opposed summary execution. Instead, at the urging of U.S. secretary of war Henry Stimson, Truman pushed for the establishment of an international tribunal to try the Nazi leaders.

The arguments for a judicial approach were compelling and soon won the day. First, judicial proceedings would avert future hostilities that would likely result from the execution, absent a trial, of German leaders. Legal proceedings, moreover, would bring German atrocities to the attention of all the world, thereby legitimizing Allied conduct during and after the war. Such proceedings would individualize guilt by identifying specific perpetrators instead of leaving Germany with a sense of collective guilt. Finally, such a trial would permit the Allied powers, and the world, to exact a penalty from the Nazi leadership rather than from Germany's civilian population.

Thus in June, July, and August 1945, representatives from the four countries gathered in London to draw up a charter for the "International Military Tribunal" to try the German civilian and military leadership for committing war crimes, waging a war of aggression, and carrying out atrocities against civilians on racial or religious grounds (known as "crimes against humanity"). Technically, the seat of the court was in Berlin, but the Palace of Justice in Nuremberg offered the best available courtroom and related facilities. Nuremberg also had symbolic value—for it was there that the Nazi Party had staged its annual mass demonstrations and that the anti-Semitic "Nuremberg Laws" had been decreed in 1935.

The fifteen negotiating sessions from June 26 to August 8, 1945, leading up to the adoption of the charter of the Nuremberg Tribunal ranged from turbulent to tumultuous. The problem was that the negotiators brought to the table their own legal conceptions and the experiences of their respective legal systems: the common-law adversarial system as it had evolved differently in England and in the United States and variations of the inquisitorial system employed in France and the Soviet Union. The task of creating an entirely new judicial entity acceptable to the four parties that blended elements from the two systems proved an incredible challenge for the negotiators. "With dissimilar backgrounds in both penal law and international law it is less surprising that clashes developed at the Conference than that they could be reconciled," wrote the chief negotiator for the United States, Robert Jackson, in his report to the president on the charter's negotiation history.

Under the inquisitorial system, most of the documentary and tes-
timonial evidence is presented to an examining magistrate, who
assembles it in a dossier, copies of which are provided to the defendant and to the court prior to trial. The court, either on its own initiative or at the request of one of the parties, will question witnesses
directly. Questioning or cross-examination by opposing counsel is a
rarity. There is no rule against hearsay evidence, which is "second
hand" testimony where a witness merely repeats what someone else
actually said. Similarly trials *in absentia,* where the accused is not
present in the courtroom, are permitted. In the Anglo-American system, in contrast, the indictment contains only a summary of the facts
alleged, and the evidence is presented in open court by the lawyers
who examine and cross-examine the witnesses. Most important,
under the adversarial system, the defendant has the right to confront
his or her accusers—a right that limits use of hearsay evidence and
written statements by witnesses who never actually come to court to
testify (*ex parte* affidavits) and requires the presence of the accused
at trial.

The charter that the negotiators eventually came up with represented a blend of the two systems. Mixing elements from both systems, the Nuremberg charter required, contrary to Anglo-American
practice, that the indictment "shall include full particulars specifying
in detail the charges against the defendants" and that there be "documents" submitted with the indictment. But, contrary to practice in
inquisitorial systems, it did not require that the prosecution present
all of its evidence with the indictment. Also contrary to such practice,
defendants could testify as witnesses in their own behalf. But in contrast to Anglo-American procedure, defendants could be compelled
to testify by the tribunal, and they were permitted to make an
unsworn statement at the end of the trial.

Finally, the negotiators agreed that the technical rules of evidence developed under the Anglo-American system of jury trials,
designed to prevent the jury from being influenced by improper or
unreliable evidence, would be unnecessary for a trial where there
would be no jury. Accordingly, the Nuremberg charter adopted the
principle that the International Military Tribunal should admit any
evidence that it deemed to have a probative value and should not be
bound by technical rules of evidence, such as the notion of
"hearsay." Commenting on the evidentiary and procedural compro-

mises, Robert Jackson wrote, "The only problem was that a procedure that is acceptable as a fair trial in countries accustomed to the Continental system of law may not be regarded as a fair trial in common-law countries. What is even harder for lawyers from a common law background to recognize is that trials which we regard as fair and just may be regarded in Continental countries as not only inadequate to protect society but also as inadequate to protect the accused individual."

Although Hitler escaped prosecution by committing suicide, twenty-two of the most notorious Nazi German leaders were tried before the Nuremberg Tribunal. After a trial that lasted 284 days, nineteen of the twenty-two defendants were found guilty, and twelve were sentenced to death by hanging.

The jurisprudence of the Nuremberg Tribunal laid the foundation for trials of over a thousand other German political and military officers, businessmen, doctors, and jurists under Control Council Law no. 10, by military tribunals in occupied zones in Germany and in the liberated or Allied nations. Major Japanese war criminals were tried before the International Military Tribunal for the Far East, whose charter was based largely on the charter of the Nuremberg Tribunal.

The Criticisms of Nuremberg

The United States chief prosecutor at Nuremberg, Robert Jackson, noted in his opening trial statement that "we must never forget that the record on which we judge these defendants today is the record on which history will judge us tomorrow. To pass these defendants a poisoned chalice is to put it to our lips as well." Given Jackson's admonition, it is ironic that history has not been altogether kind to the Nuremberg Tribunal.

Three main criticisms have been levied at the Nuremberg Tribunal: first, that it was a victor's tribunal before which only the vanquished were called to account; second, that the defendants were prosecuted and punished for crimes that had never before been defined in international law; and third, that the Nuremberg Tribunal functioned on the basis of limited procedural rules that inadequately protected the rights of the accused. These criticisms are not entirely without foundation. It was true that only victorious states were represented on the Nuremberg Tribunal. Some commentators have criticized the Allies' failure to appoint a judge from a neutral country or from Germany to the tribunal. It has been suggested that the post-Nuremberg trials administered by the German courts (including the conviction of the three defendants who had previously been acquitted by the Nuremberg Tribunal) attests to the fact that German judges could have dealt justly with the accused.

Moreover, the Nuremberg judges oversaw the collection of evidence and judged the defendants in a necessarily political arena, thereby raising questions about their ability to preside objectively over the trials. Most astonishing of all, however, was the fact that two of the judges, General Nikitchenko of the Soviet Union and Robert Falko, the alternate judge from France, had served earlier as members of the committee that drafted the Nuremberg charter and the indictments. Having written the law to be applied and selected the defendants to be tried, it is hard to believe they could be sufficiently impartial and unbiased. And yet they were insulated from attack because the Nuremberg charter stipulated that neither the court nor its members could be challenged by the prosecution or the defendants.

In addition, the four states that organized the Nuremberg Tribunal were guilty of many of the same crimes for which they charged their former adversaries. An American judge was prepared to convict German defendants for crimes against humanity despite the United States' having dropped the atomic bombs and firebombed civilian centers in Germany and Japan. German admiral Karl Doenitz was tried for violating the laws of war by conducting unrestricted submarine warfare, despite the fact that American naval forces had engaged in similar conduct throughout the war. Soviet judges, moreover, convicted defendants for waging aggressive war and mistreating prisoners despite the forcible Soviet annexation of the Baltic states and the Soviet's appalling record of treatment of prisoners of war. Most reprehensible of all, however, was the Soviet Union's insistence that the defendants be charged with responsibility for the Katyn forest massacre, in which 14,700 Polish prisoners were murdered in 1940, when the true perpetrators of this atrocity, we now know, were the Soviets, not the Germans.

Perhaps the most frequent criticism of Nuremberg is its perceived application of *ex post facto,* or retroactive laws, by holding individuals responsible for the first time in history for waging a war of aggression and by applying the concept of conspiracy, which had never before been recognized in continental Europe. One of the first to voice this criticism was Senator Robert Taft of Ohio in 1946, but it was not until John F. Kennedy reproduced Taft's speech in his Pulitzer Prize–winning 1956 book, *Profiles in Courage*, that this criticism became part of the public legacy of Nuremberg. To this day, articles appear in the popular press deriding Nuremberg as "a retroactive jurisprudence that would surely be unconstitutional in an American court."

The other major criticism was that the Nuremberg charter failed to provide sufficient due process guarantees and that those it did provide were circumscribed by several pro-prosecution judicial rulings. Such rulings were particularly troubling because the tribunal did not provide for a right of appeal. And the three Nuremberg defendants who were acquitted by the tribunal (Hjalmar Schacht, Franz von Papen, and Hans Fritzsche) fared little better than those convicted. Because of the absence of a double jeopardy provision in the Nuremberg charter, they were subsequently tried and found guilty by German national courts for the same crimes for which they were tried and found not guilty at Nuremberg.

Even Justice Jackson acknowledged at the conclusion of the Nuremberg Trials that "many mistakes have been made and many inadequacies must be confessed." But he went on to say that he was "consoled by the fact that in proceedings of this novelty, errors and missteps may also be instructive to the future."

Despite its shortcomings, the Nuremberg precedent demonstrated that the creation of an international criminal tribunal was feasible. The substantive principles of the Nuremberg charter and judgment were unanimously affirmed by the United Nations General Assembly in 1946. The concept of war crimes was further developed in the four Geneva Conventions of 1949 for the protection of war victims. The Nuremberg charter's definition of crimes against humanity contributed to the adoption in 1948 of the Convention on the Prevention and Punishment of the Crime of Genocide. But it would be fifty years before the international community was ready to create another international tribunal.

Creation of the Yugoslavia Tribunal

The United Nations Commission of Experts

In the face of reports of widespread atrocities in the former Yugoslavia following the outbreak of war in Bosnia and Herzegovina in 1992, the members of the United Nations Security Council began to take steps to hold the violators accountable. The first was a warning. Adopted on July 13, 1992, Security Council Resolution 764 stated that persons who commit violations of "international humanitarian law" in the former Yugoslavia will be held individually responsible.

The second step involved establishment of an historical record of the atrocities. This laid the foundation for future prosecutions of those perpetrators who did not heed the council's warning. On August 13, 1992, the Security Council adopted Resolution 771, which called upon states and international humanitarian organizations to submit to the council "substantiated information" in their possession concerning war crimes in the former Yugoslavia. Two months later, the Security Council unanimously adopted Resolution 780, which established an impartial Commission of Experts to assess the information submitted pursuant to Resolution 771, as well as information obtained through its own field investigations.

The United Kingdom, believing that the pursuit of war criminals might damage prospects for a peace settlement, made no secret of its preference that the commission be limited to passively analyzing and collating information that it received. The British government reluctantly agreed to the commission's investigative authority only after high-level interventions by United States officials. However, the United Kingdom managed to undermine this authority by insisting that the commission be funded from existing UN resources rather than including in the Resolution a specific budget for its work. The United States decided not to object, having insisted for years on a "zero-growth" UN budget. As a consequence, the commission took over a year to obtain alternative funding so as to conduct investigations in the field. All the while, evidence was being destroyed and memories were fading.

During its first months of operation, the Resolution 780 commission devoted its time to an analysis of the law applicable to the atrocities occurring in the former Yugoslavia, which it presented in an interim report to the secretary-general in February 1993. With a staff of fifty volunteer attorneys and law students and $800,000 in grants obtained from the Soros Foundation, the Open Society Fund, and the John D. and Catherine T. MacArthur Foundation, Commissioner M. Cherif Bassiouni of the United States set about creating the commission's documentation center and database at DePaul University's International Human Rights Law Institute. By

April 1994 the documentation center had systematically catalogued and analysed over sixty-four thousand documents and had created a computerized archive of over three hundred hours of videotape containing testimonies of individuals as well as graphic scenes of the Yugoslav conflict's carnage.

Subsequently, thirteen governments contributed a total of $1,320,631 to the commission's voluntary trust fund, enabling it to undertake thirty-four field investigations in Bosnia and Croatia under the direction of Commissioner William Fenrick of Canada. Fenrick would later become the legal adviser to the prosecutor of the International Criminal Tribunal. Commissioner Christine Cleiren of the Netherlands took on the task of organizing an investigation into rape and sexual assault. Under her direction, a forty-member all-female team of attorneys, mental health specialists, and interpreters interviewed 223 women in seven cities in Bosnia and Croatia who had been victims of or witnesses to rape. Commissioner Hanne Sophie Greve of Norway conducted an in-depth investigation into the ethnic cleansing of the Prijedor region of Bosnia. From some four hundred interviews of witnesses to the destruction there, Greve was able to document how the Serbs in Prijedor had carefully pre-pared their campaign before Bosnia declared independence on April 6, 1992. At the end of April 1994, the commission submitted its final eighty-four-page report, accompanied by twenty-two annexes con-taining thirty-three hundred pages of detailed information and analysis.

The Decision to Create the Yugoslavia Tribunal

Resolution 780, establishing the Commission of Experts, contained no reference to the creation of an international criminal tribunal. Instead, the resolution requested the secretary general of the United Nations to take account of the commission's conclusions in "any rec-ommendations for further appropriate steps." Some of the members of the Security Council hoped the 780 commission's work would eventually lead to domestic trials in the Balkans. It was thought that Ethiopia, where the international community had recently provided funding, attorneys, and judges to facilitate the prosecution of some three thousand officials of the fallen Mengistu regime, could serve as a model for this approach. But in the absence of radical changes in the governing regimes of Serbia, Bosnia, and Croatia, there was little likelihood that the Balkan states would diligently prosecute their own citizens or fairly prosecute those of each other for war crimes. While non-Balkan states could theoretically prosecute Balkan war crimes under what is known as "universal jurisdiction," it would be difficult for them to obtain custody of offenders or access to evidence. Thus, national prosecutions did not present the answer to the Balkan conundrum.

Other members of the Security Council favored less invasive accountability mechanisms such as monetary compensation for the victims and their families, a truth commission to identify perpetrators by name, and employment bans and purges (referred to as "lustration") to keep perpetrators from positions of public trust. The main argument for noncriminal measures was that they could achieve much of what prosecution seeks to accomplish—reparation, documentation, and punishment—without jeopardizing the peace process. Since none of the members of the council supported a major military intervention in the Balkans, as in Iraq in 1991, the cooperation of the leaders of the various parties to the conflict would be needed to put an end to the fighting and the violations of international humanitarian law. It would not be realistic to expect the Balkan leaders to agree to a peace settlement if they knew that following the agreement they would find themselves or their close associates facing potential life imprisonment.

Historically, amnesty or *de facto* immunity from prosecution has often been the price for peace. The Turks who were responsible for the genocidal massacre of over one million Armenians during World War I were given amnesty in the 1923 Treaty of Lausanne; the French and Algerians responsible for the slaughter of thousands of civilians during the Algerian war were granted amnesty in the Evian Agreement of 1962; Bangladesh gave Pakistanis charged with genocide amnesty in 1973 in exchange for political recognition by Pakistan. During the 1980s, the governments of Argentina, Chile, El Salvador, Guatemala, and Uruguay each granted amnesty to members of the former regimes who commanded death squads that tortured and killed thousands of civilians within their respective countries in order to facilitate a transition to democracy. To this list must be added the modern practice of the United Nations, which in the early 1990s worked to exclude from the Cambodia peace accords any mention of prosecuting former Khmer Rouge leaders for their atrocities; pushed the Mandela government to accept an amnesty for crimes committed by the *apartheid* regime in South Africa; and helped negotiate, and later endorsed, a broad amnesty for members of the Haitian military regime in order to induce them to relinquish power.

Even the experience of the World War II Nuremberg Tribunal eventually involved the bartering away of accountability as the price for German support of the Western alliance during the beginning of the Cold War. Within ten years of the Nuremberg trials' conclusion and Control Council Law number 10, all 150 of the convicted German war criminals (including several who were serving life sentences and a few who had been sentenced to death) were released from Landsberg Prison pursuant to a controversial clemency scheme. While this program removed "a diplomatic pebble" from the State Department's shoes, it had the effect of undermining the purpose of the Nuremberg Trials. In a nation-wide survey conducted by the U.S. State Department, West Germans overwhelmingly indicated that the reason for American leniency was that "they realize the injustice of the trials."

An amnesty deal might have hastened an end to the Balkan conflict, but there were several countervailing interests favoring criminal prosecution. First, the members of the Security Council, as parties to the Geneva Conventions and the Genocide Convention, may have been under a legal obligation to prosecute. Despite the initial efforts of the major powers to characterize the conflict as a civil war and to avoid the genocide label, this obligation was arguably triggered when the 780 commission issued its preliminary report, concluding that the atrocities in the Balkans could be characterized as grave breaches of the Geneva Conventions and genocide.

Each of the four Geneva Conventions of 1949 contains a specific enumeration of "grave breaches." These are war crimes committed in international armed conflict for which there is individual criminal liability and for which states have a corresponding duty to bring perpetrators to justice. Parties to the Geneva Conventions have an obligation to search for, prosecute, and punish perpetrators of grave breaches of the Geneva Conventions unless they choose to hand over such persons for trial by another state. The Commentary to the Geneva Conventions, which provides the official history of the negotiations leading to the adoption of these treaties, confirms that the obligation to prosecute is "absolute." In other words, states can under no circumstances grant perpetrators immunity or amnesty from prosecution for grave breaches of the conventions.

Like the Geneva Conventions, the Genocide Convention provides an absolute obligation to prosecute persons responsible for this "crime of crimes." Moreover, the Genocide Convention grants each of its parties the right to bring a case before the International Court of Justice against any other party when there is a dispute as to the interpretation or application of the convention. Thus, had an amnesty-for-peace deal been pursued for the Balkans in 1993, the members of the Security Council could have found themselves in the uncomfortable position of defending their actions before the World Court.

In addition to this potential legal problem, there were several practical reasons why an amnesty-for-peace deal would not have made sense under the circumstances. Failure to prosecute genocidal crimes in the Balkans, which have suffered from repeated cycles of ethnic violence and abuse going back six hundred years, would have served as a virtual license to repeat the crimes. At the same time, victims of war crimes and other atrocities might well have sought personal revenge (possibly by acts of terrorism) if no effort were made to bring those responsible for their suffering to justice.

Finally, whenever the international community gives its imprimatur to an amnesty for crimes of this magnitude there is a risk that regimes in other parts of the world will be encouraged to engage in systematic brutalities to achieve nationalist objectives. For example, the international amnesty given to the Turkish officials responsible for the Armenian massacre during World War I encouraged Adolf Hitler some twenty years later to conclude that Germany could pursue his genocidal policies with impunity. Briefing his generals at Obersalzburg in 1939, on the eve of the Polish invasion, Hitler said, "Genghis Khan had millions of women and men killed by his own will and with a gay heart. History sees him only as a great statebuilder. . . . I have sent my Death's Head units to the East with the order to kill without mercy men, women and children of the Polish race or language. Only in such a way will we win the *lebensraum* that we need. Who, after all, speaks today of the annihilation of the Armenians?" As David Matas, a Canadian expert on international law, observes: "Nothing emboldens a criminal so much as the knowledge he can get away with a crime. That was the message the failure to prosecute for the Armenian massacre gave to the Nazis. We ignore the lesson of the Holocaust at our peril."

Richard Goldstone, prosecutor of the ICTY from 1994 to 1996, has stated that the failure of the international community to prosecute Pol Pot (Cambodia), Idi Amin (Uganda), Saddam Hussein (Iraq), and Mohammed Aidid (Somalia), among others, encouraged ethnic cleansing in the Balkans. When the international community encourages or endorses an amnesty for human rights abuses, it sends a signal to other rogue regimes that they have nothing to lose by instituting repressive measures. If things start going badly, they can always bargain away their crimes by agreeing to peace.

Thus, in the conclusion of its preliminary report submitted in February 1993, the 780 commission joined a growing international chorus publicly calling for the creation of a Nuremberg-like tribunal to try persons believed to be responsible for atrocities in the former Yugoslavia. U.S. bureaucrats who had long opposed the United Nations effort to establish a permanent international criminal court were initially reluctant to support the idea of an *ad hoc* war crimes tribunal for the Balkans. But in his last days in office in December 1992, Secretary of State Lawrence Eagleburger announced, in the "naming names" speech, that the United States had identified ten suspected war criminals (including Slobodan Milosevic) who should be brought to trial before a modern-day Nuremberg Tribunal. Two months later France circulated a draft Security Council resolution in New York calling for the creation of a Yugoslavia war crimes tribunal, together with a report prepared by a committee of French jurists containing a detailed analysis of the legal issues involved in the endeavor.

Goals of the Yugoslavia Tribunal

On February 22, 1993, in Resolution 808, the Security Council decided in principle to establish an international tribunal "for the prosecution of persons responsible for serious violations of international humanitarian law committed in the territory of the former Yugoslavia since 1991." At the time of the vote on the resolution, four of the five permanent members of the Security Council delivered stirring remarks endorsing the concept of an international judicial solution to the Balkan crisis. In their remarks the permanent members articulated six distinct goals, or justifications, for the Yugoslavia war crimes tribunal.

The first of these, indicated in the French remarks, was to provide justice for the victims. As Richard Goldstone has noted, "the Nuremberg Trials played an important role in enabling the victims of the Holocaust to obtain official acknowledgement of what befell them." Such acknowledgement constitutes a partial remedy for their suffering and a powerful catharsis that can discourage acts of retaliation. According to Antonio Cassese, who served as the ICTY's first president, from 1993 to 1997, the "only civilized alternative to this desire for revenge is to render justice," for otherwise "feelings of hatred and resentment seething below the surface will, sooner or later, erupt and lead to renewed violence."

Second, as suggested by the United Kingdom's speech, the Tribunal would establish accountability for individual perpetrators. By assigning guilt to specific perpetrators on all sides, the Tribunal would avoid the assignment of collective guilt that had characterized the years following World War II and in part laid the foundation for the commission of atrocities during the Balkan conflict. "Far from being a vehicle for revenge," Antonio Cassese has explained, by individualizing guilt in hate-mongering leaders and by disabusing people of the myth that adversary ethnic groups bear collective responsibility for the crimes, "the ICTY is an instrument for reconciliation."

Third, noted the French representative, the operation of the Tribunal would deter continued perpetration of atrocities in the Balkans. Supporting this objective, David Scheffer, former United States ambassador at large for war crimes issues, has observed: "We know from experience in Bosnia that local authorities—camp commanders and temporary local officials—sometimes do what they can to improve the circumstances of those under their care once they know that the international community will investigate and punish those who fail to respect human rights standards." For Richard Goldstone, the existence of the Tribunal may have deterred human rights violations during the Croatian Army offensive against Serb rebels in August 1995. "Fear of prosecution in the Hague," he said, "prompted Croat authorities to issue orders to their soldiers to protect Serb civilian rights when Croatia took control of the Krajina and Western Slavonia regions of the country."

Moreover, the international prosecution of responsible individuals can become an instrument through which respect for the rule of law is instilled in the popular consciousness. Judge Gabrielle Kirk McDonald, who presided over the Tribunal's first trial, succinctly put it: "We are here to tell people that the rule of law has to be respected." By broadcasting televised highlights of the trials throughout Bosnia and Serbia, that message can get through directly to the citizenry. According to Richard Goldstone, "people don't relate to statistics, to generalizations. People can only relate and feel when they hear somebody that they can identify with telling what happened to them. That's why the public broadcasts of the Tribunal's cases can have a strong deterrent effect."

Fourth, according to the French representative, the Tribunal's activities would facilitate restoration of peace in the Balkans. Through its prosecutions, the Tribunal would promote the dismantling of the institutions and a discrediting of the leaders that encouraged, enabled, and carried out humanitarian crimes. There would be particular benefit to laying bare to Serbs unscathed in Belgrade the ghastly consequences of bloodcurdling nationalistic rhetoric. Even for those supporting Bosnian Serb leader Radovan Karadzic and former Yugoslav president Slobodan Milosevic, "it will be much more difficult to dismiss live testimony given under oath than simple newspaper reports," the tribunal's deputy prosecutor, Graham Blewitt, pointed out. "The testimony will send a reminder in a very dramatic way that these crimes were horrendous."

Fifth, as the United States' representative remarked, the Tribunal would develop an historic record for a conflict in which distortion of the truth has been an essential ingredient of the ethnic violence. If, to paraphrase George Santayana, a society that has not learned the lessons of the past is condemned to repeat its mistakes, then a reliable record of those mistakes must be established. Michael Ignatieff has recognized that the "great virtue of legal proceedings . . . [is] that their evidentiary rules confer legitimacy on otherwise contestable facts. In this sense, war crimes trials make it more difficult for societies to take refuge in denial—the trials do assist the process of uncovering the truth." The prosecutor at Nuremberg, U.S. Supreme Court justice Robert Jackson, underscored the logic of this proposition when he reported to President Truman that one of the most important legacies of the Nuremberg trials was that they documented the Nazi atrocities "with such authenticity and in such detail that there can be no responsible denial of these crimes in the future and no tradition of martyrdom of the Nazi leaders can arise among informed people." Similarly, in proving that war crimes, crimes against humanity, and genocide were committed, the ICTY can generate a comprehensive record of the nature and extent of violations in the Balkans, their planning and execution, the fate of individual victims, who gave the orders, and who carried them out. By carefully proving these facts one witness at a time in the face of vigilant cross-examination by distinguished defense counsel, the international trials can generate a definitive account capable of piercing the distortions generated by official propaganda, endure the test of time, and resist the forces of revisionism.

Finally, as both the United States and Russia stressed, the Tribunal would serve as a deterrent to perpetration of atrocities elsewhere around the globe. The punishment of crimes committed in the Balkans would send the message, both to potential aggressors and vulnerable minorities, that the international community will not allow atrocities to be committed with impunity. According to Richard Goldstone, "if people in leadership positions know there's an international court out there, that there's an international prosecutor, and that the international community is going to act as an international police force, I just cannot believe that they aren't going to think twice as to the consequences. Until now, they haven't had to. There's been no enforcement mechanism at all."

The Anatomy of the Yugoslavia Tribunal

On May 25, 1993, the Security Council adopted Resolution 827, approving the statute for the International Criminal Tribunal for the Former Yugoslavia, which had been drafted by the United Nations Office of Legal Affairs. Because the Tribunal was established under Chapter VII of the Charter of the United Nations, the orders for arrest, surrender, and judicial cooperation issued by the Tribunal are binding on all states. In many respects the ICTY is a vast improvement over Nuremberg. Its detailed rules of procedure, for example, represent a tremendous advancement over the scant set of rules fashioned for the Nuremberg Tribunal. The ICTY's jurisdiction is defined on the basis of the highest standard of applicable law, namely rules of law that are beyond any doubt part of customary law, to avoid any suggestion of *ex post facto–ism*. Defendants are granted a panoply of rights including the right to counsel, the right to remain silent, the right to view exculpatory evidence in the possession of the prosecutor, the right to a speedy and public trial, the right to cross-examine witnesses, and the right to appeal the judgment of the Trial Chamber to the Tribunal's Appeals Chamber.

Within just a few months of Resolution 827's adoption, the Tribunal's judges were elected, and its staff was hired. A high-tech courtroom was erected in what was once the Aegon Insurance building in The Hague, a mile down the road from the International Court of Justice, in the Peace Palace. The special features of the courtroom, where Slobodan Milosevic stands trial, include three interpreters' booths, a camera control booth, and a public gallery separated from the courtroom by a partition of bullet proof glass. The courtroom employs a range of sophisticated technological equipment. A simultaneous translation system allows viewers in the public gallery to follow proceedings in English, French, or Serbo-Croatian. Electronic stenographic equipment instantly converts the English language into text. Computer monitors on the witness, judges, and prosecution and defense tables allow the trial participants to simultaneously view documents, maps, and videotape exhibits. These can be highlighted and annotated by the witness using the same telestrator technology that television football commentators employ to diagram an instant replay.

Soon after its establishment, the Tribunal began to issue indictments of Serbs, Croats, and Bosnian Muslims for international crimes committed in the former Yugoslavia. While gaining custody of suspects was a major problem in the Tribunal's early years of operation, of the one hundred persons indicted by the Tribunal, nearly half have now been apprehended and surrendered to The Hague. These have included several generals, concentration camp commanders, and high-level political figures. But by far the most important denizen of the Tribunal's detention unit is former Serb president Slobodan Milosevic.

CHAPTER 5

The Crimes Charged: War Crimes, Genocide, and Crimes against Humanity

In mid-January 1999, as the Kosovo crisis simmered, monitors from the Organization for Security and Cooperation in Europe (OSCE) stumbled upon a massacre site at Racak, a town about twenty miles south of Kosovo's capital, Pristina. Racak had been subject to vicious ethnic cleansing of its mainly Kosovo Albanian population during 1998, and by the beginning of 1999 only 350 of its original 2,000 inhabitants were still living there. The independence seeking Kosovo Albanian guerrillas known as the Ushtria Çlirimtare e Kosovës (UÇK), or the Kosovo Liberation Army (KLA), had established a base near the town's power plant. From January 12 to 15, 1999, both guerrilla and Yugoslav government forces intensified their activities.

Led by William Walker, the OSCE's head of mission, monitors arrived in Racak on January 16 to verify reports that several civilians had been killed. A scene of horror awaited them: the bodies of some forty-five civilians were discovered, including twenty grouped together in a gully. Survivors said executions had been carried out by government forces, some of them dressed in police uniforms, others in black uniforms and ski masks. Many of the victims had multiple gunshot wounds. The investigators found bodies with their heads missing. Some looked as if they had been shot while running away.

Within days, the prosecutor for the International Criminal Tribunal for the Former Yugoslavia (ICTY), Louise Arbour, was on the ground, attempting to enter Kosovo from neighboring Macedonia for the express purpose of investigating the Racak killings. She was refused a visa by the Yugoslavian authorities. She pledged to investigate the atrocities, "with or without access to the territory."

The Racak massacre electrified international public opinion. It prompted the Rambouillet peace conference and subsequent political developments that ultimately unleashed the NATO bombing campaign. Indeed, much of the legitimacy of NATO's humanitarian intervention derived from the conviction that the governments of the Federal Republic of Yugoslavia and its internal province Serbia—including President Milosevic personally—were responsible for the killings of civilians at Racak. Now an international court will attempt to hold the principal suspects accountable.

Racak is the heart of the "Kosovo" indictment, the first directed against Slobodan Milosevic, filed by the prosecutor in May 1999, while the conflict was still underway. In October 2001, well after the arrest of Milosevic and his transfer to The Hague, the prosecutor amended the Kosovo indictment to add new facts and allegations. Moreover, she also added an entirely new indictment to the case, concerning acts committed in Croatia at the very earliest stages of the Yugoslav wars, in late 1991 and 1992. A third indictment, long promised but presented only in November 2001, addressed the wars in Bosnia and Herzegovina that began in 1992 and finished only with the Dayton Peace Agreement in November 1995.

The three indictments, taken as a whole, typify what the ICTY prosecutor has called "a campaign of terror and violence" directed against civilians throughout much of the Balkan region. The alleged purpose of the campaign was to drive Croats, Bosnian Muslims, and Kosovo Albanians from their homes in what has come to be known as "ethnic cleansing." This, it is alleged, was to facilitate the consolidation of Serb control over Kosovo and parts of Croatia and Bosnia and Herzegovina, areas the perpetrators hoped would eventually be incorporated within a "Greater Serbia."

The specific acts charged include the creation of an atmosphere of fear and oppression through the use of force, threats of force, and acts of violence, including mass killings, detention in concentration camps under inhumane conditions, looting and pillaging of personal and commercial property, destruction of cultural monuments, and persistent subjection of Croats, Bosnian Muslims, and Kosovo Albanians to insults, racial slurs, degrading acts, beatings, and other forms of physical mistreatment based on their racial, religious, and political identification.

The statute of the ICTY recognizes four distinct categories of offence: grave breaches of the 1949 Geneva Conventions, violations of the laws or customs of war, crimes against humanity, and genocide. If national criminal courts fail to convict on a serious offence, like murder, they can still fall back on "included offenses," such as assault or perhaps attempted murder. But the ICTY's jurisdiction is much more limited. Should it fail to convict on one of the four crimes listed in the statute, the defendant is released. Then national courts can still prosecute for lesser offenses without violating principles of double jeopardy.

Slobodan Milosevic faces charges in all four categories of offense listed in the ICTY statute. In the Kosovo indictment, he is jointly charged with four others, Milan Milutinovic, Nikola Sainovic, Dragoljub Ojdanic, and Vlajko Stojiljkovic. But none of the other four have been apprehended and brought to The Hague, so the trial is proceeding against Milosevic alone. The ICTY does not permit *in absentia* trials. Eventually, the other four may be brought to justice in separate proceedings.

Grave Breaches of the Geneva Conventions

The first category of offences, "grave breaches" (article 2 of the statute), consists of a list of eight specific acts that are drawn from texts in four international treaties, the 1949 Geneva Conventions, dealing with the laws of armed conflict. Virtually all countries in the world, including Yugoslavia, have ratified the Geneva Conventions. The four Geneva Conventions were adopted in the aftermath of World War II and attempted to fill many of the gaps in the laws of war that became apparent during that terrible conflict.

International criminal law was still in its infancy when the Geneva Conventions were drafted. The previous attempt at codification of "war crimes," the charter of the Nuremberg Tribunal, had focused on crimes committed by and against combatants, whereas the orientation of the Geneva Conventions was on noncombatants, specifically civilians, as well as persons who were *hors de combat* (literally, no longer combatants), such as prisoners and the wounded. The negotiators agreed to include a modest list of particularly heinous acts for which countries that ratified the Geneva Conventions would be bound to investigate, prosecute, or extradite suspects found in their territory.

At the time, it was not generally believed that acts contrary to the conventions that did not constitute grave breaches would compel any obligation to prosecute, although individual countries remained free to make such lesser violations of the conventions crimes under their own national law if they wished. Article 2 reads:

> The International Tribunal shall have the power to prosecute persons committing or ordering to be committed grave breaches of the Geneva Conventions of 12 August 1949, namely the following acts against persons or property protected under the provisions of the relevant Geneva Convention:
>
> a. wilful killing;
> b. torture or inhuman treatment, including biological experiments;
> c. wilfully causing great suffering or serious injury to body or health;
> d. extensive destruction and appropriation of property, not justified by military necessity and carried out unlawfully and wantonly;
> e. compelling a prisoner of war or a civilian to serve in the forces of a hostile power;
> f. wilfully depriving a prisoner of war or a civilian of the rights of fair and regular trial;
> g. unlawful deportation or transfer or unlawful confinement of a civilian;
> h. taking civilians as hostages.

Of the eight acts listed as "grave breaches" in the ICTY statute, Milosevic has been charged with willful killing, torture, willfully causing great suffering, extensive destruction and appropriation of property not justified by military necessity and carried out unlawfully and wantonly, and unlawful deportation or transfer of civilians.

Although the ICTY statute does not say this explicitly, according to the Geneva Conventions, grave breaches can be committed only during an international armed conflict. There have been hints in the case law of the Tribunal that this may no longer be the case, but the view still appears to be a minority opinion. Thus, Milosevic can be charged only with grave breaches of the Geneva Conventions, under article 2 of the statute, to the extent that this is with respect to an international—and not an internal—armed conflict.

Milosevic has been charged in the indictments with grave breaches for Croatia and for Bosnia and Herzegovina, but not for Kosovo. Although the arrival of NATO forces internationalized the Kosovo conflict, the prosecutor almost certainly felt that a charge of grave breaches would be inappropriate with respect to acts committed by Yugoslav forces against the Kosovo Albanian minority within the borders of a sovereign state, the Federal Republic of Yugoslavia.

Violations of the Laws or Customs of War

The expression "violations of the laws or customs of war" (article 3 of the statute) encompasses a range of acts that may be committed during armed conflict. They can involve illegal methods of war, in which case the victims are generally combatants. They can also involve civilians, who are, at least in theory, to be spared the ravages of war. This concept of "war crimes" is quite ancient, and there are records of individuals being held accountable for violating the laws or customs of war in ancient Greece, in the writings of Shakespeare, and during the U.S. Civil War.

An initial attempt at international codification of the "laws or customs of war" appears in the 1907 Hague Convention. The Treaty of Versailles, adopted after World War I, was the first international treaty to provide for prosecution of violations of the "laws and customs of war" as defined in the Hague Convention. Only a few perfunctory prosecutions were actually undertaken, involving abuses of prisoners of war and sinkings of hospital ships. The expression "violations of the laws or customs of war" is derived from the Nuremberg charter.

In the ICTY statute, the enumeration of acts that constitute violations of the laws or customs of war is open-ended. Article 3 states that the Tribunal can prosecute five specific acts:

> The International Tribunal shall have the power to prosecute persons violating the laws or customs of war. Such violations shall include, but not be limited to:

    a. employment of poisonous weapons or other weapons calculated to cause unnecessary suffering;

    b. wanton destruction of cities, towns or villages, or devastation not justified by military necessity;

    c. attack, or bombardment, by whatever means, of undefended towns, villages, dwellings, or buildings;

    d. seizure of, destruction or wilful damage done to institutions dedicated to religion, charity and education, the arts and sciences, historic monuments and works of art and science;

    e. plunder of public or private property.

Like the title of the provision, the rather archaic language in this list of crimes is drawn largely from the Nuremberg text.

The "Croatia" indictment deals with crimes that come the closest to traditional warfare. There were major military engagements between breakaway Croat forces and the Yugoslav National Army, together with paramilitaries and police units affiliated with it. The defining moments of the war, which took place in the final months of 1991, were the sieges of Dubrovnik, at the southern tip of Croatia, and of Vukovar, to the east, near the border with Serbia. In the Croatia indictment, Milosevic is charged with wanton destruction of cities or towns, or devastation not justified by military necessity; destruction or damage done to institutions dedicated to education and religion; and plunder of private or public property.

But because the statute says violations are not limited to this list ("violations shall include, but not be limited to"), the ICTY has drawn on other bodies of law for inspiration. In this respect, the most important provision is "common Article 3" of the four Geneva Conventions of 1949, so called because the text is the same in all four treaties. Common Article 3 prohibits "violence to life and person, in particular murder of all kinds, mutilation, cruel treatment, and torture." Milosevic is charged with murder, cruel treatment, and torture under this heading.

Unlike the "grave breaches" provisions of the Geneva Conventions, which are set out in a separate provision of the ICTY statute (article 2), the "violations of the laws or customs of war" text applies to noninternational armed conflict or civil war as well as to international armed conflict. Accordingly, Milosevic is charged with "violations of the laws or customs of war" with respect to the Kosovo conflict. He is also, of course, accused under this heading in the Croatia and Bosnia and Herzegovina indictments.

Another area of law that the prosecutor has drawn on to expand the scope of the concept of "violations of the laws or customs of war" is that set out in the two protocols to the Geneva Conventions, adopted in 1977. These are somewhat less widely accepted than the Geneva Conventions themselves, and many important countries, including the United States, have yet to ratify them. Still, Yugoslavia was a party to the two protocols prior to the outbreak of war in 1991, so in principle the law applied to the conflict.

The protocols were intended to update the Geneva Conventions, drawing in large part on the lessons learned in such conflicts as the Vietnam war and the various anticolonial and postdecolonization struggles that had raged in Africa and Asia since 1949. The protocols are particularly important in their attention to the protection of civilians and the prohibition of attacks on nonmilitary objectives. Protocol I addresses international armed conflict, and Protocol II deals with noninternational armed conflict. Protocol I is considerably more detailed and comprehensive, a sign of countries' lingering willingness to develop international law when it concerns interstate conflicts and their corresponding reluctance to expand it where internal or civil wars are concerned. With respect to the war in Croatia, Milosevic has been charged with "attacks on civilians," a violation of both of the protocols, and with "unlawful attacks on civilian objects," something forbidden by Protocol I.

The Croatia indictment also contains an isolated reference to "customary law" as the legal basis for a charge of "unlawful attacks on civilian objects." The prosecutor has taken the position that "customary law" in and of itself constitutes a basis for extending the scope of the concept of "violations of the laws or customs of war." Customary law is well recognized as a source of public international law, where many of the applicable rules are not set down in specific treaties but rather have emerged in the practice of interstate relations. Prosecuting crimes that are not defined in legislated texts is something that lawyers in the common law systems are well accustomed to, but it is rather a shock to those from other legal traditions where crimes must be very precisely defined in "black-letter law."

Crimes against Humanity

As with violations of the laws or customs of war, the ICTY statute lists several acts that may constitute crimes against humanity. But unlike the definition of "violations of the laws or customs of war," the list is not open-ended. Article 5 of the ICTY statute defines "crimes against humanity" as follows:

> The International Tribunal shall have the power to prosecute persons responsible for the following crimes when committed in armed conflict, whether international or internal in character, and directed against any civilian population:
>
> a. murder;
> b. extermination;
> c. enslavement;
> d. deportation;
> e. imprisonment;
> f. torture;
> g. rape;
> h. persecutions on political, racial and religious grounds;
> i. other inhumane acts.

All three indictments against Milosevic charge crimes against humanity. Of the acts listed in article 5 of the statute, seven specific crimes against humanity have been charged: murder; extermination; deportation; imprisonment; torture; persecutions on political, racial and religious grounds; and inhumane acts, including forcible transfers.

The concept of crimes against humanity emerged in 1945, as the four victorious powers, the United States, the United Kingdom, France, and the Soviet Union, made plans to prosecute Nazi leaders at Nuremberg. Originally, the Allies had planned to prosecute "war criminals." But as the trials were being prepared, it became obvious that the atrocities committed by the Nazis against their "own" population, within Germany's borders, did not fall within the traditional concept of violations of the laws or customs of war. Initially, the United Kingdom and the United States told representatives of Jewish organizations that international law did not provide for crimes committed by a government against its own people. The outrages committed against German Jews, as well as against the mentally disabled, gays and Lesbians, and Gypsies, or Roma, seemed destined to go unpunished.

Fortunately, the victorious powers changed their minds. A new category of crime was recognized, crimes against humanity. Nevertheless, the powers cautiously allowed for crimes against humanity to be prosecuted only when they were committed in the context of an international war. That way atrocities against civilians in the far-flung reaches of the British or French colonial empires, or in the Soviet Union, or even in the Deep South of the United States remained beyond the reach of international law. Here too, there has been great progress in recent years.

Crimes against humanity can be thought of as serious human rights violations, generally involving violence directed against civilians. There is usually an element of discrimination in crimes against humanity, which are often committed—as in Kosovo, Croatia, and Bosnia and Herzegovina—during ethnic conflict. But this is not a strict requirement for crimes against humanity to be charged, except in the case of "persecution." The ICTY statute makes this explicit, specifying that persecution must be on political, racial, or religious grounds.

Because they intrude so greatly into the internal affairs of sovereign states, prosecutions for crimes against humanity involve a requirement that they be committed as part of a widespread or systematic attack on a civilian population. Thus, the prosecution must establish that one of the prohibited acts—murder, for example—is committed as part of such an attack. Individual killings or other forms of assault on civilians will not generally rise to this threshold and cannot, therefore, be prosecuted by an international tribunal as crimes against humanity. Prosecution of the crime against humanity of murder, with which Milosevic and his accomplices are charged, is little different than that of violations of the laws or customs of war. But for the latter, there is no requirement that such violations be part of a widespread or systematic attack on a civilian population. Proving the widespread or systematic nature of the attack hardly seems to be a central issue in this case, given the large number of victims who are already named. The eligible victims are defined somewhat more narrowly than in the case of violations of the laws or customs of war, including only civilians and, apparently, even excluding military personnel who are not or are no longer engaged in combat.

Murder aside, crimes against humanity stigmatize a range of serious violations of human rights that might otherwise escape prosecution. Indeed, these violations are often committed under the cover of the law. The two other counts of crimes against humanity that are charged against Milosevic and his colleagues, deportation and persecution, are offenses of this type.

Deporting civilian populations has not always been an international crime. When World War II concluded, the Allies deported millions of Germans from their homes in Poland and elsewhere in Eastern Europe. This was pursuant to the Potsdam Agreement, reached between Truman, Churchill, and Stalin in mid-July 1945. The euphemism at the time for these brutal displacements of civilians from homes where they and their ancestors had lived for centuries was "population transfers." But no term better describes the odious practice than *ethnic cleansing,* a phase known to journalists and politicians but not found in international criminal law texts. Driving a civilian population from its homeland, using various means of terror, including murder, assault, rape, and pillage, fits squarely within the definition of *crime against humanity.* There will be no lack of evidence that such deportations took place in Kosovo in March and April 1999, as well as during the wars in Croatia and Bosnia and Herzegovina.

One area where judges may turn for guidance as to the legal scope of the term *deportation* is the Rome statute of the International Criminal Court. Adopted in July 1998 by a diplomatic conference, it enlarges the term slightly so as to cover "forcible transfer of population," an attempt to ensure that internal deportation is also covered. The Rome statute also specifies that *deportation* means forced displacement, without grounds permitted under international law, by means of expulsion or other coercive acts from the area in which a civilian population is lawfully present.

But the ICTY prosecutor seems to have another approach to this, treating "forcible transfer" not as a cognate of "deportation" but rather within the scope of "other inhumane acts." The prosecutor is probably uncomfortable with using the Rome statute to enrich and complete the definitions of offenses in the ICTY statute, because it was adopted after the conflicts in Croatia and Bosnia and Herzegovina. Reference to the Rome statute might leave the prosecution open to charges of retroactive prosecution. However, the judges of the ICTY have cited the Rome statute on several occasions as a guide to the scope of preexisting customary law.

The "inhumane acts" category of crimes against humanity is a kind of residual provision, allowing the scope of crimes against humanity to evolve and expand as international villains dream up new forms of atrocity. This of course raises concerns about the law's precision and may give arguments to the defense about fundamental unfairness and even retroactive prosecution. In a January 2000 judgment, the ICTY held that guidance as to the scope of "inhumane acts" could come from international human rights standards, such as those laid down in the Universal Declaration on Human Rights, of December 10, 1948, as well as by a range of human rights treaties. Examples include serious forms of cruel or degrading treatment of persons belonging to a particular ethnic, religious, political, or racial group; and serious, widespread or systematic manifestations of cruel, humiliating, or degrading treatment with a discriminatory or persecutory intent. The ICTY pointed specifically to "forcible transfer of groups of civilians," and this has undoubtedly inspired the prosecutor in drafting the Milosevic indictments. Other inhumane acts identified by the Tribunal are enforced prostitution and the enforced disappearance of persons.

As for "persecution," it is the broadest and, from Milosevic's standpoint, probably the most threatening accusation. *Persecution* covers any and all forms of inhumane behavior, even those that are not addressed by other provisions of the definition of crimes against humanity. Such forms involve infliction upon civilians of harassment, torment, oppression, or discriminatory measures. Individual forms of persecution might be rather minor in scope, such as prohibitions on access to public parks or even libraries, but taken as a whole and considering the scope and volume of the acts, they may cumulatively amount to a crime against humanity. Here, though, in contrast with the other acts of crime against humanity, a discriminatory intent must also be proven. The Rome statute provides a definition of the crime against humanity of persecution: the intentional and severe deprivation of fundamental rights, contrary to international law, by reason of the identity of the group or population.

Although international law no longer requires crimes against humanity to be committed in the context of an armed conflict, the ICTY statute does. For obscure reasons, the Security Council adopted an overly narrow definition of crimes against humanity. This complicates things for the prosecution and gives the defendants an argument to which they are not entitled under general international law. Milosevic may argue—as he will probably do with violations of the laws or customs of war—that there simply was no armed conflict at the time the alleged atrocities were committed.

The Crime of Genocide

Milosevic was not initially charged with genocide, which is the fourth category of crime listed in the statute (article 4). This was a surprise for many who had regularly heard the ethnic cleansing of Kosovo Albanians in 1999 described with the "*g* word." Eagerness to use the term *genocide* was to some extent driven by shame about the international community's failure to so identify the crime when it was committed in Rwanda in April and May of 1994. Then, the Security Council stood by, actually withdrawing United Nations troops rather than reinforcing the peacekeeping contingent, and stubbornly refused to use the term *genocide* even as it was going on in real time on international television before the eyes of the world.

Although the prosecutor had successfully prosecuted indictments of the three other categories of crime—grave breaches, violations of the laws or customs of war, and crimes against humanity—her record with genocide was not so impressive. Few of the indictments actually charged genocide. The first trial, of a Serb involved in killings in the Luka concentration camp in northwest Bosnia, led to an acquittal, in December 1999. The judges said they were unsatisfied with evidence that there had been any organized genocide, although they did not rule out the possibility that a deranged individual, acting alone, might commit the crime in a technical sense.

Still, the prosecutor continued to insist publicly that she was intending to indict Milosevic for genocide. Things began to change in a legal sense during the summer of 2001, when the prosecutor obtained her first conviction for genocide. The case dealt with the Srebrenica massacre, in which more than seven thousand unarmed Bosnian Muslim men and boys were summarily executed by Bosnian

Serb troops. The August 2001 conviction of General Krstic by the ICTY for genocide at Srebrenica encouraged the prosecutor, who accordingly adapted the long-promised indictment dealing with Bosnia and Herzegovina.

So Milosevic is also charged with genocide, but only with respect to the war in Bosnia and Herzegovina. The indictment refers specifically to Srebrenica, for which the prosecutor now has an important precedent, but also deals more generally with attacks on the Bosnian Muslim and Bosnian Croat populations, including abuses in the detention camps and executions of community leaders.

Genocide was defined in the Convention on the Prevention and Punishment of the Crime of Genocide in 1948. The text is a narrow one, reflecting the view that genocide is the "crime of crimes." It is closely related to the concept of crimes against humanity. Genocide is, many believe, the most serious form of crime against humanity, one that overlaps with the crime against humanity of persecution. Despite frequent criticisms of its restrictive scope, the 1948 convention definition has stood the test of time and appears unmodified in article 4 of the ICTY statute:

1. The International Tribunal shall have the power to prosecute persons committing genocide as defined in paragraph 2 of this article or of committing any of the other acts enumerated in paragraph 3 of this article.

2. Genocide means any of the following acts committed with intent to destroy, in whole or in part, a national, ethnical, racial or religious group, as such:

    a. killing members of the group;

    b. causing serious bodily or mental harm to members of the group;

    c. deliberately inflicting on the group conditions of life calculated to bring about its physical destruction in whole or in part;

    d. imposing measures intended to prevent births within the group;

    e. forcibly transferring children of the group to another group.

3. The following acts shall be punishable:

a. genocide;

b. conspiracy to commit genocide;

c. direct and public incitement to commit genocide;

d. attempt to commit genocide;

e. complicity in genocide.

Three of the acts listed in paragraph 2 of article 4 have been alleged against Milosevic: killing, causing serious bodily and mental harm, and imposing conditions of life calculated to destroy the group.

Cumulative Charging

The four categories of crimes listed in the statute overlap considerably. For example, it is possible to be charged with "willful killing" as a grave breach of the Geneva Conventions under article 2, "murder" as a violation of the laws or customs of war under article 3 (with reference to common article 3 of the Geneva Conventions), "killing" as an act of genocide under article 4, and "murder" as a crime against humanity under article 5. Because the four categories of offense have historical origins in various treaties and other documents that were adopted at different times and in different contexts, the language varies somewhat. But killing and murder are surely the same thing, at least to the extent that *killing* means intentional homicide, a point that has already been established in previous judgments.

In the indictment for Bosnia and Herzegovina, the prosecutor has charged Milosevic cumulatively, alleging that he committed "willful killing," "murder," and "killing," all for the same acts. For each of the four categories of offense, it is necessary to prove that the underlying intentional homicide took place. But there are additional elements to be proven. For example, "willful killing" as a grave breach of the Geneva Conventions requires proof that an international armed conflict existed, and that the victims were civilians, noncombatants, prisoners of war or wounded fighters. "Murder" as a violation of the laws or customs of war, involves establishing that there was an armed conflict, either international or noninternational. To obtain a conviction for "killing" as genocide, the prosecutor must prove it was committed within the context of the intentional destruction of a national, ethnic, racial, or religious group, in whole or in part. For "murder" to be a crime against humanity, there must be evidence of its widespread or systematic nature, and the crime must be directed against a civilian population.

The prosecutor may fail with one charge and succeed with another. There is nothing unusual in a prosecutor's attempting to convict on a number of related charges, and the practice is well established in the ICTY. In a domestic legal system, prosecutors often charge a shoplifter with theft and possession of stolen goods; if the theft charge cannot be made out, there may still be enough evidence for a conviction of possession. To take a more serious example, a person accused of intentional homicide may ultimately be convicted of only manslaughter (that is, negligent or involuntary homicide) if convincing evidence of the intentional nature of the killing cannot be produced.

But what happens if there is enough evidence to convict on more than one of the overlapping charges within the ICTY's jurisdiction? When this has happened, the judges have tended to enter a conviction for the more "specific" of the offenses and acquit for the other charges. The more "specific" ought also to be the more "serious," but the judges have been reluctant to establish a hierarchy among the statute's four categories of offense. They are thus likely to consider genocide to be more "specific" than crimes against humanity, for example. But even if they convict for more than one offense with respect to the same facts, because the two crimes do not truly overlap, they will impose the sentences to be served concurrently rather than consecutively. Thus, a person sentenced for the same acts to seven years for grave breaches of the Geneva Conventions and to ten years for crimes against humanity will serve ten years, not seventeen years.

Criminal Participation

The actual definitions of the crimes are only part of the issues addressed by the indictments. The prosecutor must also prove the manner in which each crime was committed. In the context of ordinary criminal law, most prosecutions target the principal offender, such as the person who pulls the trigger. But international criminality is a form of organized crime, and the most serious of the offenders is usually several steps removed from the battlefield.

The ICTY statute says, in article 7(1), that the four categories of crime can be committed by a person who "planned, instigated, ordered, committed or otherwise aided and abetted in the planning, preparation or execution of a crime." In the case of genocide, it is also possible to commit the crime by "conspiracy." With respect to grave breaches of the Geneva Conventions, article 2 uses the words "committed or ordering to be committed." ICTY case law has added another form of complicity or participation, known as "joint criminal enterprise." Accordingly, a person may be convicted for acts that were physically committed by others, even those of which the accused was unaware at the time, to the extent that they were logical and reasonable consequences of a more general criminal enterprise.

The "joint criminal enterprise" approach is at the core of the prosecution's strategy. The indictments allege that the physical acts were largely committed by Yugoslav armed forces and police. If it can be established that Milosevic ordered these units to commit crimes, then he can be convicted of them even if the crimes were actually committed—in a physical sense—by others. There is nothing unusual here; virtually all criminal law systems recognize that an individual who abets or incites another to commit a crime that is actually committed is himself or herself guilty of that same crime.

Obtaining proof that Milosevic actually gave orders may not be a simple matter. It is said that the Nazis bequeathed a glorious paper trail of their atrocities, but Hitler himself left very few documentary records. The same may be the case in Yugoslavia. Certainly there is nothing in the indictment charging that on a specific date Milosevic gave an order to deport or persecute the Bosnian Muslims, Bosnian Croats, or Kosovar Albanians. Prosecution lawyer Geoffrey Nice has said publicly that he will produce in evidence "telephone intercepts" of conversations between Milosevic and the Bosnian Serb leader Karadzic, but he has not said what the intercepts contain. If enough evidence can be produced of criminal acts, carried out over a protracted enough period of time, and without any measures having been taken by the authorities to deter or punish those responsible, judges might be willing to convict Milosevic based on circumstantial evidence. They would have to be convinced that there is no other plausible explanation. The only way such atrocities could have been committed would be that they were officially ordered or sanctioned at the highest levels of the government.

Command or Superior Responsibility

Even if the prosecutor has trouble proving Milosevic ordered or sanctioned international crimes, there is an alternative. The statute allows a conviction based on "command responsibility," which is a form of criminal responsibility applied to military and civilian leaders when there is not enough evidence that they actually gave orders to commit war crimes and crimes against humanity. The statute says that, when a crime has been committed by a subordinate, the superior can also be convicted of the crime if he or she knew or had reason to know that the subordinate was about to commit or had committed such an act and the superior failed to take the necessary and reasonable measures to prevent such an act or to punish the perpetrator. Command responsibility was first used in a controversial trial before a United States military commission of the Japanese commander whose troops sacked Manila in the final stages of World War II. General Yamashita appealed to the U.S. Supreme Court, but a majority agreed that the conviction should be upheld, and his execution went ahead. What was then a controversial basis of prosecution has since achieved virtually universal recognition. The legitimacy of the principle of command responsibility as a basis for prosecuting civilian and military leaders was confirmed in the Rome statute of the International Criminal Court, adopted in July 1998, six months before the Racak massacre. The ICTY has already obtained several convictions based on command responsibility.

The indictments allege that Milosevic had either *de jure* (that is, by law) or *de facto* (in fact) authority over a range of military and civilian institutions within the governments of Serbia and the Federal Republic of Yugoslavia. The strength of the claims progresses over the decade of the 1990s, culminating in the Kosovo indictment. Accordingly, the Croatia indictment notes that Milosevic exercised control over the "Serbian Bloc" through the presidency of the Socialist Federal Republic of Yugoslavia in 1991 and 1992, acting through two of his "agents," Borisav Jovic and Branko Kostic. The "Bloc" commanded the Yugoslav National Army as well as militia units. The indictment also charges that Milosevic exercised effective control of the military counterintelligence section known as the KOS (Kontraobavestajna sluzba). Finally, Milosevic is alleged to have "exercised control" over several key officials in the Serb government, including ministers and deputy ministers.

By the time of the Kosovo events, Milosevic had been elected president of the Federal Republic of Yugoslavia and as such was president of the Supreme Defense Council. By virtue of this position, he also exercised authority over police units during a state of imminent threat of war or a state of war. A declaration of imminent threat of war was proclaimed on March 23, 1999, and a state of war on March 24, 1999. As for his *de facto* authority, this is said to flow from his leadership position in the Socialist Party of Serbia, over which Milosevic presided throughout the 1990s.

The prosecutor makes more cautious claims with respect to the war in Bosnia and Herzegovina. After the formal withdrawal of Yugoslav forces in May 1992, this war was waged at least ostensibly by autonomous Bosnian Serb forces. The indictment notes that as a member of the Supreme Defence Council Milosevic "exercised substantial influence and control over other members of the Council." This is probably not enough to establish command or superior responsibility. Moreover, it is nowhere alleged that he exercised the same level of "substantial influence and control" over Radovan Karadzic, Ratko Mladic, Biljana Plavsic, Momcilo Krajisnik, and others in the Bosnian Serb civilian administration and military.

CHAPTER 6

Dramatis Personae

The trial of Slobodan Milosevic involves a colorful mosaic of personalities from throughout the world: judges, lawyers, witnesses, and participants. We briefly describe some of the key figures here.

The Judges

Milosevic is being tried by Trial Chamber III of the International Criminal Tribunal for the Former Yugoslavia (ICTY), which is presided over by Richard May, assisted by Patrick Robinson and O-Gon Kwon.

Richard George May, an Englishman, practiced criminal law as both prosecutor and defense counsel before being appointed a full-time judge in 1987. Early in his career, he ran for the Labour Party in elections to the House of Commons. Judge May joined the Tribunal in 1997 and has sat in several of its landmark cases, including *Furundzija* and *Kupreskic*. Even before the trial of Milosevic actually began, in February 2002, May had several public skirmishes with the defendant in pre-trial proceedings. May was firm and more than once showed some impatience. Milosevic may well succeed in regularly getting under his skin in the course of the trial, with unpredictable results.

Patrick Lipton Robinson is the international lawyer of the three, a former deputy solicitor general in the Jamaican Attorney

General's Department, although he also has very significant criminal law experience. Judge Robinson joined the Tribunal in 1998. He has been a member of the United Nations International Law Commission, the Haitian Commission on Truth and Justice, as well as the Inter-American Commission on Human Rights, which he chaired in 1991.

A newcomer to the ICTY, Judge **O-Gon Kwon** was elected to the ICTY in 2001 by the UN General Assembly. Previously, Judge Kwon was senior judge at the Taegu High Court and throughout his career has held a number of senior judicial positions within the Republic of Korea, several of which have been in the field of criminal law.

The case has already been to the Appeals Chamber once, on a successful application by the prosecutor seeking a joint trial on all three indictments, which Trial Chamber III had refused. The composition of the five-judge Appeals Chamber changes regularly, and it is likely that the bench which heard the first appeal will not be the same to consider an eventual appeal from conviction or sentence or from acquittal, depending on the result of the trial. As now constituted for the Milosevic case, the Appeals Chamber is presided over by Claude Jorda, and includes Theodor Meron, Fausto Pocar, Mehmet Güney, and David Hunt.

The president of the Appeals Chamber, **Claude Jorda,** is a French magistrate, formerly prosecutor-general at the Paris Court of Appeals, who has been with the Tribunal almost since its beginning, in 1994. He became its president in 1999 and has worked at streamlining its operations and expediting its proceedings. **Theodor Meron** is an American academic, formerly Charles L. Denison Professor of Law at New York University Law School and a renowned specialist on human rights, humanitarian law, and Shakespeare. Prior to his election to the Tribunal in 2001, Meron worked as a counselor in international law for the United States Department of State, something Milosevic might raise in an attempt to disqualify him or impeach his impartiality. **Fausto Pocar** is an Italian academic, a professor at the University of Milan, with a distinguished profile in international human rights. For more than a decade before joining the Tribunal in early 2000, Pocar was a member of the Human Rights Committee, the treaty body responsible for implementing the International Covenant on Civil and Political Rights. He chaired the committee from 1990 to 1991. Australian judge **David Hunt** joined the Tribunal in 1998 after a distinguished career as a barrister, judge, and law reformer with a specialty in the area of criminal law. Judge Hunt issued the first indictment against Milosevic in May 1999. **Mehmet Güney,** of Turkey, who was actually elected as a judge for the sister International Criminal Tribunal for Rwanda, is the fifth member of the Appeals Chamber assigned to the Milosevic case, at least for the purposes of the pretrial appeal. Judge Güney is above all an international lawyer, and he was a member for many years of the UN International Law Commission. The composition of the Chamber may change by the time the trial is over and the appeal of conviction and sentence or of acquittal is filed.

The Prosecution

The prosecutor, **Carla Del Ponte,** has played a very active personal role in the Milosevic case, sometimes donning a gown and making legal arguments herself before the judges. A Swiss national, Del Ponte was appointed to the ICTY in 1999, picking up the baton from Canadian Louise Arbour, who stepped down one year before the end of her term. Del Ponte had a fierce reputation as a prosecutor in Switzerland, handling many celebrity cases, including several directed against the Russian mafia.

The senior trial attorney, charged with making the opening statement and overseeing the actual courtroom work, at least for the Kosovo portion of the trial, is a folksy, down-to-earth prosecutor from southern British Columbia, Canada, **Dirk Ryneveld.** Coordinating the prosecution case with respect to the genocide charges, in Bosnia and Herzegovina, is a British queen's counsel, **Geoffrey Nice.**

Behind the scenes will be a senior legal advisor, Canadian **William Fenrick,** a former military lawyer and the same person who advised prosecutor Del Ponte not to proceed any further on investigating allegations of NATO war crimes in 1999. Also close to the action will be Deputy prosecutor **Graham Blewitt,** an Australian who cut his teeth doing domestic war crimes prosecutions and someone who has been with the ICTY since its beginning. Other prosecution lawyers who have appeared before the Tribunal in the Milosevic case include **Hildegaard Yertz-Retzlaff, Darryl Mundis** and **Norman Farrell.**

Now retired from the Tribunal, former prosecutor **Louise Arbour** will never be too far from the proceedings. To much international media attention, she stood on the borders of Kosovo in early 1999, after being denied an entry visa, and warned Milosevic of prosecution. Then in May 1999, after obtaining issuance of the indictment, an international arrest warrant, and a seizure order and after ensuring that all Tribunal personnel had left the Kosovo area where they might be exposed to some form of reprisal, she declared to international media that for the first time in history a sitting head of state, Slobodan Milosevic, had been indicted for crimes against humanity and war crimes by an international tribunal. A few weeks later, Arbour announced her resignation, and she left the Tribunal shortly afterwards to assume a seat on the Supreme Court of Canada. Perfectly fluent in the two official languages of the Tribunal, English and French, Arbour was a professor of criminal law before being appointed to the Canadian judiciary in the 1980s.

Another keen observer, and almost sure to be a frequent media commentator on the proceedings, is **Richard Goldstone,** now a judge of the South African Constitutional Court but prosecutor of the ICTY from 1994 to 1996. Judge Goldstone launched the first prosecutions before the ICTY and was responsible for indicting Bosnian Serb leaders Radovan Karadzic and Ratko Mladic in July 1995. At the time, many charged that by going after leaders of one of the warring parties he might fatally compromise any attempts at a negotiated peace. But the indictment signaled the beginning of the end for Karadzic and Mladic. Within months a peace agreement had been initialed at Dayton, not by Karadzic and Mladic, who were afraid to leave Bosnia precisely because of the indictment, but by the man they mandated to represent their interests, Slobodan Milosevic.

The Defense

Milosevic has refused to appoint counsel, insisting upon acting in his own defense. "The lawyer who defends himself has a fool for a client," goes the old saying, but Milosevic may be the exception that makes the rule. To be fair to him, he has shown considerable talent as an advocate and defends himself with great aplomb and imagination, challenging the prosecutor's case on a basic technical level while all the time using the courtroom as a political stage.

Several lawyers have emerged to take up his case, some of them apparently having some form of authorization from the accused, others evidently freelancing. One who has spoken on behalf of the accused at press conferences in The Hague is Belgrade lawyer **Zdenko Tomanovic.** Tomanovic has teamed up with Serb colleagues like **Dragan Krgovic** and **Dragoslav Ognjanovic,** who represent Milosevic's wife, **Mirjana Markovic.** The three have acted on behalf of Milosevic and his family with respect to corruption charges before the Yugoslav courts.

But the most visible defense counsel is American lawyer **Ramsay Clark,** who has previously acted for defendants before the International Criminal Tribunal for Rwanda. Son of a U.S. Supreme Court justice, Clark was attorney general of the United States under President Lyndon Johnson. But since those days, he has made a career of aggressively challenging U.S. foreign and domestic policy, from the bombing of North Vietnam and Iraq to the detention of Taliban prisoners in Cuba and practically everywhere in between. Together with British lawyer **John Livingston,** Clark has apparently obtained visiting privileges and has been authorized to spend time advising Milosevic in his cell in the Tribunal's detention facility in Scheveningin, a suburb of The Hague.

Others who have sought the limelight include French lawyer **Jacques Vergès,** notorious for his defense of everyone from left-wing terrorists like Carlos the Jackal to Nazi war criminal Klaus Barbie. A Canadian lawyer associated with the remains of that country's Communist Party, **Christopher Black,** has also been a frequent advocate on Milosevic's behalf. Black too has already acted on behalf of genocide defendants at the International Criminal Tribunal for Rwanda. Two Dutch lawyers, **Nico Steijnen** and **Erik Olof,** have also been involved in the Milosevic case.

The *Amici Curiae*

Three lawyers have been designated by the registrar, with the approval of the Trial Chamber, to assist the Tribunal as *amici curiae* (literally, friends of the court). They make representations before the Tribunal, particularly on legal issues, so that both sides of the case are properly aired even if there is no formal defense as such. In November 2001 they filed a pretrial motion, subsequently dismissed by the Trial Chamber, raising several of the issues to which Milosevic has alluded in his courtroom statements: illegal composition of the Tribunal, bias, and illegal rendition from Yugoslavia to The Hague. The *amici* are even entitled to cross-examine witnesses during the trial.

Mischa Wladimiroff is a senior Dutch criminal lawyer and university professor who has been noted for his expertise in commercial and economic crime. **Richard Kay** is an English barrister. The two acted on behalf of the ICTY's first important defendant, Dusko Tadic, until he fired them well into the case. But while on the file, they litigated some of the most significant questions about the Tribunal's existence. The pair have also been involved as defense counsel before the International Criminal Tribunal for Rwanda. The third *amicus* is Belgrade lawyer **Branislav Tapuskovic.** A specialist in financial and juvenile crimes, Tapuskovic is also the chair of Serbia's bar association and is highly regarded by the profession. Previously, he represented Zdravko Mucic, a Bosnian Croat, but like his colleagues, Tapuskovic was fired during trial.

The Witnesses

Many of the very specific acts alleged in the indictment—the Srebrenica massacre of 1995, for example—will have to be proven in court by eyewitness and other testimony. In many cases, this will not be for the first time, but as a general rule the Trial Chamber in the Milosevic trial may have to go through the exercise one more time. In previous decisions, the ICTY has refused to take "judicial notice" of such "facts" as the existence of an armed conflict or its qualification as international or noninternational, holding that these had to be established by evidence in each individual trial. But one of the rules of procedure and evidence adopted recently by the judges allows them to "admit a transcript of evidence given by a witness in proceedings before the Tribunal which goes to proof of a matter other than the acts and conduct of the accused." In previous cases, they have relied on transcripts from other trials in order to expedite proceedings and might well do the same thing in the Milosevic case.

One of the state security chiefs who worked under Milosevic, **Rade Markovic,** is thought to be high on the prosecution's witness list. Markovic is currently serving a prison sentence in Belgrade for abuse of office and is also facing Yugoslav justice for his alleged involvement in an unsuccessful assassination attempt on opposition leader Vuk Draskovic. Markovic has not been publicly indicted, nor is he named in the Milosevic indictments as a member of the "joint criminal enterprise."

Another whose cooperation the prosecution is seeking is **Zoran Lilic,** who served as president of the Federal Republic of Yugoslavia before Milosevic succeeded him in 1997. Lilic told a Belgrade news magazine, *Vreme*, that he had been one of Milosevic's closest friends until they had a falling out in 1998 about the behavior of Serb police in Kosovo. "Until now I have not agreed to testifying," he said in the *Vreme* interview, "even though I have had many reasons for doing so because of personal grievances, because of what has been done to me, my family and my safety."

The prosecutor has apparently been courting **Radislav Krstic,** who was the first person to be convicted of genocide by the Tribunal, in August 2001. Krstic served with the Bosnian Serb armed forces under General Ratko Mladic and was implicated in the Srebrenica massacre of July 1995. His sentence of forty-six years, currently under appeal, was the stiffest ever handed out by the Tribunal. The prosecutor might be offering the prospect of a significant reduction of the jail term in return for his cooperation. The Tribunal will mitigate sentences in return for "substantial cooperation with the prosecutor," although Krstic should know that the prosecutor can make no guarantees and that any reduction in his sentence will have to be endorsed by the judges.

On Milosevic's side, he has himself given no indication of who might be called in defense. However, one of his legal advisors, Zdenko Tomanovic, has said Milosevic will call leading NATO political officials and other international personalities. Milosevic's remarks indicate some of the lines of his defense: NATO aggression against Serbia, Kosovar terrorism, and the hypocrisy of Western leaders who treated him as a peacemaker at Dayton in 1995 only to turn on him later as the conflict's villain since its beginning. Whether the judges consider these issues even to be germane to the charges is doubtful, but should they see a connection, Milosevic will be entitled to require the personal attendance and testimony of appropriate witnesses. Theoretically, at least, these could include: **Richard Holbrooke,** the U.S. diplomat who piloted the negotiations at

Dayton in 1995; former U.S. president **Bill Clinton** and current United Kingdom prime minister **Tony Blair,** who were the political leaders of the Kosovo bombing campaign and the negotiations that preceded it; and **Javier Solana,** NATO secretary-general during the Kosovo campaign.

Milosevic might also attack the fairness of the proceedings on the grounds of prosecutorial mischief. Why did it take ten years for the prosecutor to launch an indictment concerning the war in Croatia? The argument may have some validity if Milosevic can show the prosecutor acted vexatiously. But how would he do this? Might he insist on questioning former prosecutors **Louise Arbour** and **Richard Goldstone?** The judges of the Trial Chamber might be uncomfortable refusing Milosevic the right to explore the issue.

But with all of these "celebrity" witnesses, Milosevic will be taking a chance that is well-known to experienced trial lawyers. It is always dangerous to call a witness when you do not know what he or she will testify in evidence. The results are unpredictable and may do more harm than good to the lawyer's case.

The Alleged Partners in Crime

The three indictments against Milosevic name a long list of what might be called his alleged coconspirators, or rather, the partners in the "joint criminal enterprise" that he is alleged to have directed. In some cases it is also claimed that they were his subordinates, an allegation that exposes Milosevic to conviction on the grounds of command responsibility. In effect, under article 7(3) of the ICTY statute, as their commander or superior he can be held responsible for their crimes "if he knew or had reason to know that the subordinate was about to commit such acts or had done so and the superior failed to take the necessary and reasonable measures to prevent such acts or to punish the perpetrators thereof." The alleged partners in crime can be divided into three groups, corresponding to each indictment and also, in a general sense, to the historical evolution of the Serb leadership elements over the 1990s.

Members of the "joint criminal enterprise" during the 1991–95 period consist of a number of senior military officials, including General **Veljko Kadijevic,** who was federal secretary for national defence, General **Blagoje Adzic,** chief-of-staff of the Yugoslav

National Army, General **Aleksandar Vasiljevic,** who was responsible for the military counterintelligence service *Kontraobavestajna sluzba* (KOS). All three were retired in 1992. Kadijevic and Adzic are living in Belgrade. Kadijevic has published a book about the war. Vasiljevic was arrested on charges of divulging official secrets, but in 1999 Milosevic appointed him deputy head of military security.

Civilian officials include **Jovica Stanisic,** chief of the intelligence service (Drzavna bezbednost or DB) of the Republic of Serbia and once described as Milosevic's "right hand man." Now retired in Belgrade, he was recently reported to be the "first honorary member" of the new Serbian Social Democratic Party, founded by Zoran Lilic. One of Stanisic's key subordinates, **Franko Simatovic,** was head of the special operations component of the DB known as "Franko's guys."

Others in the circle included **Tomislav Simovic,** minister of defense of the Republic of Serbia, as well as **Branko Kostic** and **Borisav Jovic,** a former Milosevic aid. Jovic later denounced Milosevic, claiming his former boss had pulled a "fast one" with the alleged withdrawal of Yugoslav troops from Bosnia in 1992. Simovic and Jovic are retired, the latter living near Kragujevac, although he recently founded a new political organization, the Democratic Socialist Party. Kostic lives near Cetinje and teaches at Podgorica University.

Many of the atrocities in Croatia and, later, in Bosnia and Herzegovina were committed by volunteer Serb militias. One of the groups, the Serbian Volunteer Guard, famously known as the "Arkanovci," or "Arkan's Tigers," was headed by the notorious Arkan, **Zeljko Raznatovic.** Arkan was killed in a hail of bullets in the Belgrade Inter-Continental Hotel in January 2000. Another group, known as "chetniks" "*Šešeljevci*" or "Seselj's men," was led by **Vojislav Seselj,** who also served as president of the Serbian Radical Party. Seselj remains an active player in Serb politics and is a deputy to both the Serbian and the Yugoslav parliaments.

Several local officials within Serb-dominated areas of Croatia are alleged to have been involved in the atrocities, including **Milan Martic, Milan Babic,** and **Goran Hadzic.** Martic headed the Serb puppet state in the Krajina, in eastern Croatia, in 1991. He has been indicted by the ICTY since 1995. Martic has been reportedly living in Banja Luka, in the Republika Srpska. Babic, another Krajina official, is said to be lying low in Belgrade. When Milosevic fell, Babic tried to revive the Serb Democratic Party. Goran Hadzic another Krajina boss, settled in Novi Sad, where he took up a position as councilor to the director general of the Serbian Oil Industry, a position he apparently still occupies.

At the apex of the leadership of the Bosnian Serbs during the war stood **Radovan Karadzic** and **Ratko Mladic.** Both men were indicted by the ICTY in July 1995 for war crimes, crimes against humanity, and genocide for their overall conduct of the war. Although they remained at large, the direct consequence of their indictment was that they did not travel to Dayton for the peace negotiations. Instead, they mandated Milosevic to reach agreement on their behalf. A second indictment charged them with complicity in the Srebrenica massacre of July 1995.

A psychiatrist by training, Karadzic was president of the Serbian Democratic Party of Bosnia and Herzegovina (SDS). In March 1992 he became president of the Bosnian Serb National Security Council. A few weeks later, he was elected president of the three-member presidency of the Republika Srpska. In December 1992 Karadzic was elected president of the Republika Srpska, a position he retained until shortly after the Dayton negotiations in November 1995. By mid-1996 he had fallen from power, succeeded by Momcilo Krajisnik at the head of the Republika Srpska, although for some time it was suspected that he continued to play an important role behind the scenes. He is now said to be in hiding in Han Pijesak, in eastern Bosnia, protected by a strong contingent of bodyguards in the event that United Nations SFOR troops attempt to arrest him. Rumors circulate periodically that he will be brought to The Hague or even surrender voluntarily. Reports vary as to whether Karadzic continues to play a significant role in Bosnian Serb political life.

Ratko Mladic is a career soldier in the Yugoslav army who was stationed in Macedonia and Kosovo before the wars. He was appointed commander of the 9th Corps (Knin Corps) of the Yugoslav People's Army (JNA) in June 1991 and participated in the fighting in Croatia. With the rank of major general, in May 1992 he assumed command of the forces of the JNA's Second Military District in Sarajevo. When the Yugoslav army formally withdrew from Bosnia and Herzegovina in May 1992, Mladic stayed behind as commander of the main staff of the Bosnian Serb forces (VRS). He held the position as military leader of the Bosnian Serbs until after Dayton. Mladic is now living in Banovo Brdo, a wealthy suburb of Belgrade.

In 1996 the ICTY held a form of preliminary hearing concerning the indictments of Karadzic and Mladic, although they were not present. Three judges concluded:

> The uniform methods used in committing the said crimes, their pattern, their pervasiveness throughout all of the Bosnian Serb–held territory, the movements of prisoners between the various camps, and the tenor of some of the accuseds' statements are strong indications tending to show that Radovan Karadzic and Ratko Mladic planned, ordered or otherwise aided and abetted in the planning, preparation or execution of the genocide perpetrated in the detention facilities.

Convincing evidence of Karadzic and Mladic's involvement in the Srebrenica massacre was also presented to the Tribunal. Since then, the specific role of Mladic in Srebrenica has been thoroughly documented by the Tribunal in its conviction of one of his subordinates, General Krstic.

The United States negotiator at Dayton and during its buildup, Richard Holbrooke, in his book *To End a War,* described the relationship between Milosevic and his erstwhile allies in Bosnia as tense and difficult. Far from being the mob boss in charge of a couple of undisciplined capos, Milosevic had an uneasy partnership with Mladic and Karadzic, Holbrooke has suggested. The prosecutor may argue otherwise. Significantly, however, while the prosecutor has claimed that Karadzic and Mladic were members of the "joint criminal conspiracy," she does not seem to be arguing that they were "subordinates" of Milosevic.

Closely associated with Karadzic, **Momcilo Krajisnik** was president of the Republika Srpska National Assembly, a member of the Bosnian Serb National Security Council, and an SDS leader. He is in custody at the ICTY detention facility in Scheveningin. Another high-ranking SDS official, **Biljana Plavsic,** took over the Republika Srpska presidency following the formal withdrawal of Karadzic from public life, in July 1996. Plavsic surrendered to the ICTY in January 2001 and was released on bail later in the year. Both are now awaiting trial, which is scheduled to begin sometime in 2002.

The insiders change by the time of the Kosovo events, in 1999, for which four others are indicted together with Milosevic. **Milan Milutinovic** was president of Serbia during the period. A lawyer by training, Milutinovic was part of the Yugoslav political structure, holding a variety of positions. He became the minister of foreign affairs of the Federal Republic of Yugoslavia in August 1995 and was elected president of Serbia in December 1997. **Nikola Sainovic** was an SPS leader who held a succession of ministerial posts, including prime minister of Serbia and then deputy prime minister of the Federal Republic of Yugoslavia, from 1994 to 1998. Designated by Milosevic to be his representative for Kosovo, Sainovic chaired the commission for cooperation with the Organization for Security and Cooperation in Europe Verification Mission in Kosovo, in late 1998, and was an official member of the Serbian delegation at the Rambouillet peace talks in February 1999. **Vlajko Stojiljkovic,** also an SPS functionary, served as minister of internal affairs of Serbia during the period covered by the Kosovo indictment. Both Sainovic and Stojiljkovic are still members of the federal Yugoslav parliament, where the majority is not sufficiently strong to lift their immunity from prosecution.

Colonel General **Dragoljub Ojdanic** was a career soldier in the Yugoslav National Army. During the war in Bosnia and Herzegovina, Ojdanic commanded the Uzice Corps, which was involved in actions in eastern Bosnia. Later he served as chief of the General Staff of the First Army of the Armed Forces (VJ) of the Federal Republic of Yugoslavia. In November 1998 Milosevic appointed him chief of the General Staff, a position he held through the first half of 1999. He is protected by the military, and it is feared that any attempt to arrest him might provoke a revolt.

CHAPTER 7

The Rules of the Road: Procedure before the International Tribunal

The statute of the International Criminal Tribunal for the Former Yugoslavia (ICTY) gives little guidance as to the procedural rules the Tribunal is to apply. The United Nations Security Council delegated this question to the judges themselves in article 15 of the ICTY statute: "The judges of the International Tribunal shall adopt rules of procedure and evidence for the conduct of the pre-trial phase of the proceedings, trials and appeals, the admission of evidence, the protection of victims and witnesses and other appropriate matters." Some 125 specific rules of procedure and evidence were adopted by the Tribunal's judges on February 11, 1994. Amended frequently since then, these rules address a broad range of procedural and evidentiary issues and have tended to evolve with the Tribunal's developing experience and expertise.

The ICTY judges decided to embrace a largely adversarial approach to their rules of procedure, rather than that of the inquisitorial system prevailing in continental Europe. Yet there were four significant deviations from the adversarial system: first, as at Nuremberg, there is no rule against hearsay evidence. Second, plea bargaining and granting of immunity were not included. Third, in order to protect witnesses from retaliation, their identities may under certain circumstances be withheld from the accused notwithstanding the defendant's right of confrontation. And fourth, the prosecutor may appeal a Trial Chamber's judgment of acquittal on grounds of error of law or error of fact.

Hearsay Evidence

The relatively liberal use of hearsay testimony has proven to be somewhat controversial. Hearsay evidence is indirect evidence whereby a witness does not testify about what he or she actually saw but rather about what someone else told the witness. Fundamentally, it is rejected by courts because of its inherent unreliability and because of the difficulty of assessing the credibility of an eyewitness who is not in court. Moreover, if the person who has personal knowledge of a given fact, rather than secondary or indirect knowledge, does not testify, then that person cannot be cross-examined in order to assess the validity of the evidence. As the U.S. Supreme Court has stated, "face-to-face confrontation generally serves to enhance the accuracy of fact-finding by reducing the risk that a witness will wrongfully implicate an innocent person." Hearsay testimony is seen as unreliable also because the out-of-court asserter has not made a solemn oath or declaration before a judicial authority. In contrast, if he or she were to testify to these matters under oath before the Tribunal, the witness would be more aware of the solemn nature of the proceedings, the importance of testifying truthfully and accurately, and the possible legal consequences of failure to testify or to do so truthfully (up to a year's imprisonment and a $10,000 fine, according to the Tribunal's rules of procedure and evidence).

An affidavit or sworn declaration is a form of hearsay evidence because the witness does not actually appear in court. Rather, a written document prepared by the witness is presented in lieu of live testimony. The existence of the oath or declaration at the end of the document is believed to enhance its reliability.

The Tribunal's judges have rejected these arguments about hearsay evidence on the ground that, as professional judges, as opposed to lay jurors, they are perfectly capable of assessing the appropriate weight and credibility of such statements. Fundamentally, the reason behind the common law's relatively inflexible approach to hearsay evidence has been to ensure that lay jurors would not be unduly influenced by evidence that judges themselves knew, from experience, to be frail and unreliable. Even common law jurisdictions, particularly in proceedings where there are no juries, have become increasingly less rigid on the subject. At Nuremberg, of course, much reliance was placed on affidavit evidence and other forms of hearsay.

The importance of affidavit and other hearsay evidence in the Milosevic trial should not be exaggerated. The prosecutor has said she expects to call hundreds of witnesses, many of whom may testify on facts that are relatively uncontroversial. To that extent, the trial of Milosevic will be considerably more like a traditional common law trial than were the Nuremberg proceedings.

Compelling Testimony

One of the weaknesses of the Tribunal's rules, as interpreted by the Appeals Chamber in the 1997 *Blaskic* decision, is that the Tribunal may issue subpoenas only to individuals acting in a private capacity. The Tribunal does not have the authority to subpoena persons acting as government officials to testify either for the prosecution or the defense. While the Tribunal may order states to produce official witnesses, it is for the state to decide which official to produce. Cooperation with such an order is enforceable only by the Security Council. That body has shown itself singularly uninterested in intervening to assist the Tribunal. Above all, it is particularly unlikely to use its power in any matter involving the permanent members of the council—the United States, the United Kingdom, the Russian Federation, China, and France—because of the veto power held by these states.

The Tribunal's 1997 ruling thus makes it unlikely that current and former Western leaders, including Bill Clinton, Madeleine Albright, or Richard Holbrooke, will end up testifying as defense witnesses in the Milosevic trial. But because prosecutors are expected to call high-ranking Serb officials for their case, the judges, in using a fairness principle enshrined in the rules known as "equality of arms," may decide that Western countries have to allow someone of equal stature to testify for Milosevic. The judges know that if no high-level Western officials come to testify, it will only play into Milosevic's strategy of trying to discredit the proceedings.

As an alternative to ordering the appearance of a witness, the Tribunal can authorize the taking of a deposition or permit the witness to appear via live videoconference. In either case, the other party has the right to attend and cross-examine the witness. In past cases, the Tribunal has stressed the general rule that a witness must physically be present at the Tribunal. Deposition and video-link evidence will be permitted only where "the testimony of the witness is shown to be sufficiently important to make it unfair to proceed without it and that the witness is unable or unwilling to come to the Tribunal." Further, the Tribunal has said that the evidentiary value of depositions and video-link testimony will be considered "not as weighty as evidence produced in the courtroom."

Anonymous Witnesses

The use of anonymous witnesses by the Tribunal in its early stages engendered a heated debate in the academic literature. After the Tribunal first permitted such testimony, former U.S. Department of State legal adviser Monroe Leigh argued, in an editorial published in the *American Journal of International Law,* that the right to examine or cross-examine witnesses guaranteed by the Yugoslavia Tribunal statute cannot be effective without the right to know the identity of adverse witnesses. "It is a radical proposition to suggest that the minimum rights of the accused to a fair trial can be diminished in order to protect witnesses and victims," Leigh concluded. Even the Tribunal's deputy prosecutor, Graham Blewitt, confided that he was "personally very uncomfortable with the notion of going forward with witnesses whose identities are not disclosed to the accused." Such use of anonymous witnesses would be held unconstitutional in a U.S. court and raises serious questions about the fairness of the proceedings. More acceptable means of protecting witnesses include using voice and image–altering technology and withholding the witness's name from the public record. When such persons testify, the blinds that separate the public gallery from the courtroom will be closed.

It is unlikely that the prosecutors will rely on anonymous witnesses in the Milosevic case. In recent years, the Office of the prosecutor appears to have dropped the practice in favor of less extreme forms of witness protection.

Plea Bargaining

The absence of plea bargaining has also been a point of contention. Plea bargaining is used in some common law jurisdictions to expedite proceedings. The accused in effect negotiates with the prosecution, agreeing to plead guilty, often to a lesser charge than the ones listed in the indictment. The two sides, defense and prosecution, make common submissions to the court on the appropriate charges and the fit sentence. Plea bargains are often offered in return for cooperation with the prosecution, such as testimony against accomplices in crime.

Judges generally endorse such plea bargains on the assumption, usually well placed, that any agreement between defense and prosecution probably reflects a fair and accurate assessment of the facts and the legal issues. But critics of plea bargaining argue that it can distort the judicial search for truth and that vulnerable defendants may often plead guilty to crimes for which they may have been acquitted had a full trial taken place. It is also claimed that the prosecution does not faithfully enforce the law when it plea-bargains, because it accepts guilty pleas for lesser crimes in order to spare the burden of holding a trial.

To induce accused war criminals to testify against higher-level officials, the United States proposed a provision to be included in the rules of procedure and evidence that would have allowed the prosecutor to grant full or limited immunity in exchange for an accused's cooperation. In arguing for its proposal, the United States said: "we recognize that many other legal systems have difficulty with these concepts, but we believe that these tools would be helpful in the war crimes context for leading prosecutors up the chain of command from the foot soldier who directly committed an atrocity to the military or political leader who had knowledge of or commanded it."

The first president of the Tribunal, Antonio Cassese responded: "The persons appearing before us will be charged with genocide, torture, murder, sexual assault, wanton destruction, persecution and other inhuman acts. After due reflection, we have decided that *no one* should be immune from prosecution for crimes such as these, no matter how useful their testimony may otherwise be." Yet, in a partial concession to the U.S. position, the Tribunal agreed that cooperation is a factor to be taken into account in imposing sentence. Since Judge Cassese stepped down from the presidency of the Tribunal and was replaced by the U.S. judge Gabrielle Kirk McDonald, the judges have begun to permit the prosecutor to drop charges against low-level individuals who provide critical cooperation. This is an important development because testimony of Milosevic's comrades (the so-called "insiders") may prove to be the key to successful prosecution in this case. But the prosecutor may have to pay a price for such cooperation.

Double Jeopardy

In contrast to the rule against double jeopardy as applied by United States courts, the Yugoslavia Tribunal permits the prosecutor to appeal an acquittal. As the U.S. Supreme Court has said, "Perhaps the most fundamental rule in the history of double jeopardy jurisprudence has been that a verdict of acquittal . . . could not be reviewed, on error or otherwise, without putting [a defendant] twice in jeopardy, and thereby violating the Constitution." The proscription of the double jeopardy clause in the U.S. Constitution applies no matter how erroneous or ill-advised the trial court's decision appears to the appeals court. The rationale for the American rule is that "to permit a second trial after an acquittal, however mistaken the acquittal may have been, would present an unacceptably high risk that the Government, with its vastly superior resources, might wear down the defendant so that 'even though innocent, he may be found guilty.'"

This rationale is just as applicable to prosecution before an international criminal court as to domestic prosecutions. The Yugoslavia Tribunal's Office of the prosecutor, together with state authorities assisting that office, will have the full resources of the court and several interested states behind it, whereas defendants and their counsel have minimal resources at their disposal.

The rule against appeals by the prosecutor is, however, unique to American jurisprudence. Other common law countries, including Canada and the United Kingdom, permit their prosecutors to bring such appeals. Further, use of the American rule would contravene the Tribunal's function of bringing uniformity to the prosecution of Yugoslav war criminals and the application of international criminal law.

Judicial Notice

Finally, the Tribunal's rules permit the judges to take judicial notice of "facts of common knowledge." Judicial notice is a technique by which judges accept certain facts as not needing proof because of their notoriety. To take an obvious and banal example, no court would require proof that the sun rises in the east and sets in the west. The Tribunal has agreed that the April 1992 declaration of independence by Bosnia and Herzegovina and its subsequent recognition by the United States and the countries of the European Union need not be proven and can be assumed.

But the Tribunal has held that "it is necessary for the Tribunal as a criminal tribunal to be more conservative with regard to judicial notice than the International Court of Justice might be with regard to civil litigation between governments." The Tribunal has further held that it will not take judicial notice of the factual findings of reports of United Nations bodies, including the UN Commission of Experts for the former Yugoslavia. Nor will the Tribunal take judicial notice of findings of fact made in previous cases before the Tribunal. This means, in the absence of stipulations by the defense, that the prosecutor will have to start from scratch in proving the history and character of the Yugoslavia conflict, as well as Milosevic's involvement. For example, in order to convict Milosevic of grave breaches of the Geneva Conventions for atrocities in Bosnia, the prosecutor will have to prove that the conflict in Bosnia was an international armed conflict rather than merely a civil war between Bosnian Serbs, Bosnian Croats, and Bosnian Muslims. This is why the trial of Slobodan Milosevic is expected to last over two years.

There is one exception to this principle, on which the prosecutor may attempt to rely. It is possible for the prosecution to introduce transcripts of testimony from previous trials. This will be allowed only where Milosevic and the defendant in the earlier trial had essentially the same interests and where the witness was properly cross-examined.

The Steps of the Proceedings

Proceedings before the ICTY are initiated when the prosecutor issues an indictment. This is submitted to the judge who has been designated to review indictments for that particular month. If the judge confirms the indictment, an arrest order or order for the transfer of the accused is sent to the authorities of the state in which the accused is located. After arrest, the accused is transferred to the Tribunal's

Detention Center at the Hague. Immediately upon arrival, he or she is brought before a Trial Chamber and formally charged.

Before trial the prosecutor must disclose relevant evidence to the defense. This procedure is well recognized in common law jurisdictions and is mandated by the principle of a fair trial. The defense should never be taken by surprise at trial. Above all, it is essential to inform the defense of evidence that may be favorable to his or her case. The Tribunal departs from common law practice in imposing certain disclosure requirements on the defense as well. To this extent, the proceedings before the ICTY borrow aspects from inquisitorial approaches used by courts in continental Europe and many other parts of the world. In reality, because of Milosevic's noncooperation, many of these pretrial requirements were not followed to the letter.

At trial, both sides may begin with an opening statement. Should the defense prefer, the right to make an opening statement may be reserved until after the prosecutor has finished presenting his or her evidence. After the parties' opening statements, the prosecutor presents evidence, essentially by calling witnesses. Such witnesses may testify as to what they have personally seen or heard, or they may produce material objects or, in exceptional cases, hearsay statements or other secondary evidence on behalf of other witnesses. Expert witnesses may also be called to give opinions about such matters as cause of death, trajectories of firearms and so on. For example, the prosecutor will require experts in order to establish that the mortar shell attack on the Sarajevo marketplace in February 1994 came from Serb-held positions.

Each prosecution witness may be cross-examined by counsel for the defense after he or she has testified, and then may be re-examined by the prosecutor. Cross-examination is not a feature of continental legal systems, and many defense lawyers from non-common-law backgrounds have shown themselves to be rather clumsy with the process. Not so Slobodan Milosevic, who, from the first days of the trial, has shown himself to be a skilled cross-examiner.

Some evidence is off-limits for the prosecution. For example, the prosecution has no right to call the defendant as a witness. The defendant has a right to silence. This means that not only can the defendant not be required to testify but the defendant's silence cannot be used to suggest that he or she may have something to hide.

This principle, which is well-established in the case law of many national systems and also a principle of international law, is really counterintuitive. Judges and juries all assume that an innocent person will want to give his or her version of the facts. The issue is unlikely to arise in this case, however. Given his posture before the Tribunal, it would seem likely that Milosevic will relish his personal testimony as a high point in the proceedings. It may indeed prove to be a duel between prosecutor and accused of grand proportions and with unpredictable results.

When the prosecutor has finished calling evidence, her case will be formally closed. Then Milosevic will be entitled to make a motion for acquittal. Such motions are regularly filed but rarely granted. They can be allowed only when the prosecutor has failed to produce any evidence to substantiate an essential element of the case. In ruling on a motion to acquit, it is not for the judges to weigh or assess the credibility of the evidence.

Upon dismissal of a motion to acquit, the defense must then decide whether to present evidence. The defense can call witnesses, just like the prosecution, including experts to challenge any opinions ventured by prosecution witnesses. It is at this point that the defendant decides whether to testify in his or her own defense. The prosecution may cross-examine the defense witnesses, including the defendant himself. When cross-examination is completed, the defense has a right to reexamine witnesses, essentially to clarify matters that were raised for the first time during the cross-examination.

At the close of the case for the defense, the prosecutor may present rebuttal evidence to respond to issues raised initially in defense. There is a still more limited right for the defense to bring evidence to counter such rebuttal evidence. Theoretically, such a process could go on forever. But once the defense has answered the prosecutor's rebuttal evidence, the evidentiary phase of the trial is over, unless the judges themselves wish to call witnesses.

The judges can play a relatively active role in the proceedings, although this varies depending upon their personalities and above all their judicial backgrounds. Under the common law, trial judges play a largely passive role in the proceedings. They are there to arbitrate between prosecution and defense, who bear the primary responsibility for decisions about what evidence to produce. Under the inquisitorial system, the trial judge directs the proceedings, which are conceived of not as a duel between two lawyers but rather as a search for objective truth. The ICTY proceedings strike a balance between these two philosophies. Accordingly, the judges can themselves require that evidence be produced. Moreover, they may intervene regularly during the proceedings in questioning witnesses and raising issues that prosecution and defense may not have adequately developed.

Under common law proceedings, the issue of sentencing is not addressed until there has been a determination of guilt. In part this is because juries usually rule not on the punishment that may be imposed but on whether the facts establish the guilt of the accused beyond a reasonable doubt. At the sentencing phase, the defendant may wish to produce evidence "in mitigation," that is, a variety of factors tending to show that, despite a finding of guilt, he or she ranked rather low on the scale of evil. For obvious reasons, it could be unfair to require the defendant to produce such evidence before the jury at the trial stage, as it might prejudice any finding of guilt or innocence.

This is not the case before the ICTY. Any evidence that is relevant to sentencing is to be produced before the completion of the trial's evidentiary phase. This works in both directions. The prosecutor may produce evidence of Milosevic's "bad character" just as the accused may do the opposite. Perhaps Milosevic will want to call former United States negotiator Richard Holbrooke, who was often charmed by the Serb leader, at this stage.

After the presentation of evidence, the two sides make their closing arguments. Thereafter, the Trial Chamber deliberates *in camera* (in private) and pronounces its findings in public. There is no rule of unanimity for the three judges. If two of the three judges determine that the defendant is guilty beyond a reasonable doubt, then a conviction will be entered and a sentence imposed.

An appeal may be lodged within fifteen days of the judgment by either the prosecution or defense. The possible grounds of appeal are limited to an error on a question of law that invalidates the decision or an error of fact that has occasioned a miscarriage of justice. The Appeals Chamber may grant or dismiss the appeal or even revise the Trial Chamber's decision. Sometimes, where sentencing issues are involved, the Appeals Chamber will return the case to the Trial Chamber for a new or revised determination.

It is possible for both sides to introduce new evidence at the appeal stage, though the circumstances where this is allowed are limited. More likely in such cases is what are called "review proceedings." When a new fact has been discovered that was not known at the time of the proceedings and that could have been a crucial factor in reaching the decision, the convicted person or the prosecutor may apply for review of the judgment. It is possible to seek review even of a decision of the Appeals Chamber.

Finally, sentences are served in one of the countries that have indicated to the Security Council their willingness to accept convicted persons. Previously convicted persons have spent time in the prisons of Norway and Germany on this basis. It is expected that the ICTY will go out of existence by about the year 2015, and many of those it has convicted are likely to be still serving sentences at that time. The ICTY statute therefore provides that the rules governing imprisonment are those of the state where the sentence is being served. European states generally opt for a relatively clement prison regime. The death penalty has, of course, been abolished throughout European countries. They eschew long sentences and many of them—this was the case for Yugoslavia before its breakup—do not even allow for life imprisonment. In any case, they are relatively generous in allowing prisoners to apply for conditional release or parole.

If they were not, they would likely find themselves challenged before human rights bodies like the European Court of Human Rights. Indeed, when all of the appeals and applications for revision are concluded, if Milosevic is convicted, the final court before which he may appear is the Strasbourg-based European Court of Human Rights. It applies the European Convention on Human Rights, an international treaty that enshrines such principles as the right to be free of "inhuman or degrading punishment." Although the European Court of Human Rights has never made a formal ruling on the issue, the court would be likely to consider a sentence of life imprisonment without some form of reasonable parole eligibility to constitute "inhuman or degrading punishment." Moreover, the case law of the European court over its forty-year history has grown increasingly more liberal. Even punishment deemed acceptable by contemporary standards may no longer meet the test in future decades.

CHAPTER 8

Real Justice or Realpolitik: Can Milosevic Get a Fair Trial?

There were disquieting echoes of Nuremberg at the arraignment of Slobodan Milosevic in The Hague on July 3, 2001. Standing before the three-judge panel, Milosevic challenged the validity of the Security Council–created International Criminal Tribunal for the Former Yugoslavia (ICTY). "You are not a judicial institution; you are a political tool," Milosevic protested to the Tribunal's judges. Drawing on the widely accepted notion that the post–World War II Nuremberg trials were tainted by "victor's justice," Milosevic's initial trial strategy was to attempt to discredit the ICTY's legitimacy and impartiality. Prior to the start of the trial, one of Milosevic's legal advisors, former United States attorney general Ramsey Clark, widely circulated a draft brief (including Milosevic's handwritten notations) attacking the Tribunal. Ramsay Clark has been involved for some time at the International Criminal Tribunal for Rwanda, where he has made similar essentially political attacks on the court's very existence.

Will history remember Milosevic as a victim of victor's justice, a scapegoat tried in a show trial before a one-sided court? Or will the Milosevic trial be seen as fair and free of political influence? More than anything else, the answer to these questions may dictate the ultimate success or failure of the proceedings.

On the one hand, if viewed as legitimate, the trial of Slobodan Milosevic can potentially serve several important functions in the Balkan peace process. By focusing the issue of responsibility for the decade of war and atrocity on Milosevic and disclosing the way the Yugoslav people were manipulated by their leaders into committing acts of savagery on a mass scale, the trial can help break the cycle of violence that has long plagued the Balkans. While this will not completely absolve the underlings for their acts, it may make it easier for victims eventually to forgive or at least to reconcile with former neighbors who were caught up in the institutionalized violence. The trial can also promote a political catharsis in Serbia, enabling the new leadership to distance itself from the discredited nationalistic policies of the past. The historic record generated from the trial can help to educate the Serb people, long subject to Milosevic's propaganda, about what really happened in Croatia, Bosnia and Herzegovina, and Kosovo, and help to ensure that such horrific acts are not repeated in the future.

On the other hand, a trial seen as "victor's justice," will undermine the goal of fostering reconciliation between the ethnic groups living in the former Yugoslavia. The historic record developed by the trial will forever be questioned. The trial will add to the Serb martyrdom complex, merely another in centuries of grievances, all requiring vengeance. The judicial precedent will also be tainted. For any real advance to be made in the long march toward the establishment of a permanent international criminal court, Milosevic's trial must be seen to be more about real justice than realpolitik.

The Legitimacy of the Yugoslavia Tribunal

In his initial pretrial appearances, Milosevic essentially confined his comments to contesting the legitimacy of the Tribunal. He said, for example, that it was illegally constituted and that it should have been established by the United Nations General Assembly. While the Nuremberg charter precluded challenges to the legitimacy of the Nuremberg Tribunal itself, the International Criminal Tribunal for the former Yugoslavia considered the question in its first case, in 1995. The Tribunal ruled that, although its creation by the Security Council was without precedent, it was a valid product of the Security Council under the council's broad powers to take action to maintain international peace and security. The Tribunal did not settle definitively the question of whether the General Assembly could create such a court, but it did rule that in the circumstances there could be no doubt about the Security Council's power to do so. The Security Council was acting pursuant to the authority granted by the Charter of the United Nations in matters of international peace and security, and the ICTY found no grounds to quarrel with its exercise of such power.

Still, it is a bit late in the day for Milosevic to be challenging the Tribunal on this ground. After all, he recognized the legitimacy of the Tribunal when he signed the Dayton Agreement in 1995. Article X of the Agreement on the Military Aspects of the Peace Settlement, which is an annex to the Dayton Agreement, states: "The Parties shall cooperate fully with all entities involved in implementation of this peace settlement, as described in the General Framework Agreement, or which are otherwise authorized by the United Nations Security Council, including the International Tribunal for the former Yugoslavia." Any doubt should have been erased when Milosevic authorized the transfer of Drazen Erdemovic as a material witness before the Tribunal in connection with the Srebrenica massacre and evidence he might have as to the involvement of Radovan Karadzic and Ratko Mladic.

In response to Milosevic's challenges to the Tribunal's legitimacy at a pretrial hearing in August 2001, Presiding Judge Richard May said, "Mr. Milosevic, we are not going to listen to these political arguments." But later in the year, the *amici curiae* lawyers appointed by the Tribunal raised the same issue in a pretrial motion. On November 8, 2001, the Trial Chamber assigned to the case dismissed this challenge to its legitimacy: "In the Chamber's view, the establishment of the International Tribunal with power to prosecute persons responsible for serious violations of international humanitarian law in the former Yugoslavia, and with the obligation to guarantee fully the rights of the accused, is, in the context of the conflict in the country at that time, pre-eminently a measure to restore international peace and security. Accordingly, it fell squarely within the powers of the Security Council to create the institution." The issue can, of course be raised on appeal, but this will happen only after the trial is completed.

The Trial Chamber also rejected a suggestion that another court should be called upon to rule on the ICTY's legitimacy. The *amici curiae* revived an old argument by which the ICTY judges themselves can hardly be expected to rule impartially on their own existence. As Milosevic may point out, the judges who made that decision could not be seriously expected to decide the issue impartially, given that their incredibly prestigious, $150,000-per-year jobs hinged on the outcome. An alternative might be to seek an "advisory opinion" from the International Court of Justice, the supreme judicial organ of the United Nations and the ICTY's neighbor in The Hague. The ICTY itself has no power to request an advisory opinion of the international court, but this step could be taken by either the Security Council or the General Assembly. If such an opinion were sought, however, the result would seem easy to predict. In a February 2002 decision dealing with an unrelated matter, the judges of the International Court of Justice referred to the ICTY and appeared to endorse its legitimacy.

Milosevic has also attempted to attack the legitimacy of the Tribunal before other courts. Because the Tribunal is located in the Netherlands, on the outskirts of The Hague near the beach resort town of Scheveningin, Dutch courts seemed worth a try. But The Hague District Court refused to entertain Milosevic's challenge, saying it lacked jurisdiction. This is a reasonable conclusion, given that the Tribunal is an international body that reports to the UN Security Council. The ICTY statute states quite unequivocally that the 1946 Convention on the Privileges and Immunities of the United Nations applies both to the Tribunal and to its employees.

Milosevic has also taken a claim to the European Court of Human Rights, based in Strasbourg. The European court applies the European Convention on Human Rights, a major human rights treaty that sets out the basic principles of judicial independence, the presumption of innocence, and fundamental due process rights. Over the more than forty years of its operation, it has developed a sophisticated body of case law on fair trial issues. The European convention applies to the Netherlands, of course, and the European Court has sometimes ruled against the Dutch government on justice issues. But as with the domestic Dutch courts, Milosevic is unlikely to get the European Court of Human Rights to even hear his argument. The European Convention on Human Rights applies only to matters subject to the jurisdiction of European states. The court will almost surely rule that the International Criminal Tribunal, created by the UN Security Council, is simply not subject to the jurisdiction of the Netherlands.

Victor's Justice

If Milosevic's goal is not to obtain a dismissal but to discredit the Tribunal, he may have a greater chance of success with his argument that the Yugoslavia Tribunal, like the Nuremberg Tribunal, represents "victor's justice." In contrast to the Nuremberg Tribunal, however, the Yugoslavia Tribunal was created neither by the victors nor by the parties involved in the conflict but rather by the United Nations, representing the international community of states. The judges of the Yugoslavia Tribunal come from all parts of the world and are elected by the UN General Assembly, in which each of the 189 member states has an equal vote. Moreover, the message of the International Tribunal's indictments, prosecutions, and convictions to date of Muslims and Croats, as well as Serbs, has been that a war crime is a war crime, whoever committed it. The Tribunal has taken no sides.

The decision to establish the Yugoslavia Tribunal, however, was made by the UN Security Council, which cannot truly be characterized as a neutral third party; rather, it has itself become deeply involved and taken sides in the Balkan conflict. The Security Council has imposed sanctions on Milosevic's Serbia, which it felt was most responsible for the conflict and atrocities. Throughout the conflict, the Security Council was quite vocal in its condemnation of Serb atrocities, while criticisms of those committed by Muslims and Croats were comparatively muted. And most problematic of all, three of the council's permanent members—the United States, France, and the United Kingdom—led the seventy-eight-day bombing campaign against Milosevic and Serbia in 1999.

While both the prosecutor and the judicial chambers of the Tribunal were conceived to be independent from the Security Council, the fact that the council selects the Tribunal's prosecutor cannot be overlooked. The judges are selected by the General Assembly from a short list proposed by the Security Council, and they have to stand for reelection after a four-year term. Moreover, the Tribunal's operation has depended on hundreds of millions of dollars of contributions from the United States and its Western allies. And much of the staff of the Office of the prosecutor is on loan from NATO countries. Although a creature of the United Nations, the Tribunal has, according to its former president, Antonio Cassese, tended to "take into account the exigencies and tempo of the international community." There are those who would argue that this means that the Tribunal has yielded to the objectives of the United States and other NATO powers without whose financial and military support the Tribunal could not function.

The Timing of the Indictment

For evidence of the political influence of the United States on the Yugoslavia Tribunal, Milosevic can turn to the suspicious timing of his indictment. It was issued on May 22, 1999, sixty days into the NATO bombing campaign against Serbia. The indictment came down at a crucial time when popular support for the intervention was waning in several NATO countries in the face of intense press criticism of NATO's use of cluster bombs and depleted-uranium munitions; attacks on civilian trains, truck convoys, and media centers; and the accidental bombings of the Chinese Embassy in Belgrade and the territory of neighboring Bulgaria. If this bad press forced a premature end of the bombing campaign, American officials feared that it might irrevocably damage NATO's credibility, potentially leading to its demise.

One of the lingering questions about the decision of the Office of the prosecutor to charge Milosevic with crimes, including genocide, relating to the wars in Bosnia and Herzegovina and in Croatia is why it took so long to issue an indictment. After all, talk about claims of his involvement in the alleged atrocities had persisted since 1991 and 1992. It was, in fact, such allegations that led to the establishment of the ICTY by the Security Council in May 1993, following the recommendation by the Commission of Experts. Yet for years, the United States appears to have pressured the Tribunal's prosecutor not to indict the Serb leader, whose cooperation was seen as essential for the Balkan peace process.

As war raged in Kosovo in early 1999, nongovernmental organizations and journalists called upon the prosecutor to indict Milosevic. After all, the case for the NATO intervention's legitimacy was based upon the fact that major human rights violations against the Kosovo Albanian minority had already been committed and were continuing. So why was the man in charge, Slobodan Milosevic, not already indicted? Rumors circulated that prosecutor Louise Arbour was still seeking evidence to link him with various atrocities, such as the

January 1999 massacre at Racak. She allegedly visited the world's major capitals in order to wrest evidence out of the hands of reluctant spymasters. And then the United States changed its mind. It suddenly began pressing for the immediate issuance of charges against Milosevic, knowing that such action would bolster the political will of NATO countries to continue the bombing campaign and would ultimately force Milosevic to accept NATO's terms for Kosovo. After years of refusing to turn over sensitive intelligence data to the Tribunal in order to protect "sources and methods," the United States and Britain were hurriedly handing over reams of satellite imagery, telephone intercepts, and other top secret information to help the prosecutor make the case against Milosevic. That the prosecutorial agenda was being influenced by the intelligence services of the main NATO powers is certainly a disturbing situation, although it would be a major innovation for the Tribunal to conclude that this is enough to call into question the prosecutor's impartiality.

Another question Milosevic may raise regarding the Kosovo indictment concerns the personal situation of prosecutor Louise Arbour. A senior Canadian judge, she had taken leave to assume the ICTY prosecutorship in mid-1996. By early 1999, following the unexpected retirement of a member of the Supreme Court of Canada, it was widely rumored that she would be appointed to her country's most senior judicial body. Canada is, of course, a member of NATO and was an active participant and enthusiastic supporter of the Kosovo bombing campaign. Within a few weeks of indicting Milosevic, Louise Arbour resigned from the ICTY following her appointment to the Supreme Court of Canada. Milosevic may argue that there is more than a whiff of impropriety when the prosecutor, who is a national of one of the belligerent parties, indicts the president of the other side and is then, literally within days, named to a plum position.

On numerous occasions before and after the first Kosovo indictment, in May 1999, prosecutor Louise Arbour and then her successor, Carla Del Ponte, stated that there were ongoing investigations and that Milosevic might still face justice for pre-1996 charges. These would concern the more than three year-long war in Bosnia and Herzegovina, as well as the briefer but brutal war when Croatia declared its independence in 1991. Although the indictments avoid even hinting at an explanation for the delay, it may be that evidence considered essential to the prosecutor became available only after Milosevic's fall, in late 2000. The prosecutor may have hesitated also because she was unsure about how the Tribunal would handle the charges. She is now more sure of herself in light of some recent rulings in other cases.

Yet Milosevic is entitled to be tried without delay. Justice delayed, goes the old saw, is justice denied. But the authorities generally disregard what is called "precharge delay," unless it can be shown that there was real abuse by investigators or prosecutors. The clock that governs the right to a speedy trial begins to tick only with the start of actual proceedings, or at any rate with the arrest and arraignment. As a result, Milosevic has no serious argument based on the delay in actually bringing the charges, unless he can establish some vexatious aspect of the prosecutor's behavior.

Should Milosevic challenge the prosecutor's impartiality, she may answer that it is the Tribunal that must be impartial and that, even if he succeeds in establishing some misconduct by the prosecution, this cannot be enough to compromise the right to a fair trial. Yet there are already precedents by the *ad hoc* tribunals for intervention by the judges when the prosecutor has misbehaved. In a dramatic and controversial ruling, the ICTY's sister tribunal dealing with the Rwandan genocide ordered that an accused be freed and that the prosecutor be prevented from renewing the charges because of inexcusable delay and other conduct it considered abusive. The decision was later rescinded, but the principle by which the judges can order a case not to proceed when there is "abuse of process" by the prosecutor remains. Milosevic will be sorely tempted to exploit this avenue of defense, especially as it contributes to his contention that the Tribunal amounts to nothing more than political persecution.

Nevertheless, questions raised by *amici curiae* lawyers about the prosecutor's independence were resoundingly dismissed by the Trial Chamber in November 1999. "In this case, there is not a scintilla of evidence advanced either by the accused or by the *amici curiae* to support the contention of any *mala fides* or abuse of power on the part of the prosecutor in issuing an indictment against the accused," wrote the three judges. They noted that the fact that the prosecutor may have been inspired by Security Council resolutions to develop the case was "no different from a government in a domestic jurisdiction setting a prosecutorial policy." The judges did suggest, however, how Milosevic might succeed in challenging the prosecutor's independence:

What would impugn her independence is not the initiation of investigations on the basis of information from a particular source, such as the Security Council, but whether, in assessing that information and making her decision as to the indictment of a particular person, she acts on the instructions of any government, any institution or any person. There is no suggestion that the prosecutor acted upon the instructions of any government, any body, or any person in her decision to indict the accused.

Head-of-State Immunity

Historically, a head of state enjoyed immunity from criminal charges issued by another sovereign state. But the immunity came to an end in the Treaty of Versailles, in 1919, which pledged to try the German emperor. Likewise, the charter of the Nuremberg Tribunal specifically provided that there would be no immunity for heads of state. So that there would be no mistakes in The Hague, the Security Council once again reiterated the principle in article 7 of the ICTY statute: "The official position of any accused person, whether as Head of State or Government or as a responsible Government official, shall not relieve such person of criminal responsibility nor mitigate punishment."

Milosevic himself does not seem to have put much stock in head-of-state immunity, though it was raised by the *amici curiae* in their pretrial motion. The judges were unimpressed, noting that there was no support for the suggestion in customary international law. They referred to recent developments, like the decision of the English House of Lords to deny such immunity to the former Chilean leader Augusto Pinochet, as well as the exclusion of head-of-state immunity in the statute of the International Criminal Court, adopted in July 1998. The International Court of Justice, in a February 2002 ruling, made it clear that international law recognized no such immunity before international criminal tribunals like the ICTY.

The Manner of Milosevic's Surrender

The newly elected president of the Federal Republic of Yugoslavia, Vojislav Kostunica, backed up by a Yugoslav federal court ruling, refused to permit the extradition of Milosevic to The Hague. But in a late-night move that caught everyone off guard, Kostunica's political rival, Serbian prime minister Zoran Djindjic, instructed the Serb police under his command to take Milosevic secretly to a U.S. air base in Tuzla, Bosnia, from which Milosevic was transferred by military jet to The Hague on July 28, 2001. In announcing the action, Djindjic said that he had been forced to take a "difficult but morally correct" decision to protect the interests of Serbia (that is, the United States and its European allies were promising $1.28 billion in aid if Serbia surrendered Milosevic). Immediately thereafter, a furious Kostunica protested that the extradition of Milosevic was "illegal and unconstitutional."

Meanwhile, on board the flight to The Hague, Milosevic reportedly told the Tribunal officials who read him his rights, "You are kidnapping me, and you will answer for your crimes." In analogous cases (*Stocke v. Germany* [1991] and *Bozano v. France* [1986]), the European Court of Human Rights held that luring or abduction in violation of established extradition procedures is a human rights violation for which dismissal of the charges is the appropriate remedy. But the ICTY rejected the argument in the *Dokmanovic* case on the ground that there does not exist a formal extradition treaty between the International Criminal Tribunal for the Former Yugoslavia and the Federal Republic of Yugoslavia. Moreover, the "vertical" relationship between the Tribunal and states is to be contrasted with the "horizontal" relationship between two states. The *amici curiae* have challenged aspects of the Milosevic surrender, claiming they constitute "abuse of process." Rejecting the argument, the Trial Chamber held that any irregularities in Milosevic's surrender were not in any event "an egregious violation" of his fundamental rights.

Whatever the technical legal merits of his argument, politically, the timing of Milosevic's surrender could not be worse for the Tribunal. He arrived at the Yugoslavia Tribunal on St. Vitus's day, the solemn holiday commemorating the Serbs' defeat by the Ottoman Turks at the battle of Kosovo Polje, in 1389, which figures so prominently in the Serb mythology of victimization.

Unclean Hands

Milosevic may point out that Franjo Tudjman, the former leader of Croatia, was never indicted by the Tribunal for the mass atrocities that Croatian troops committed against the Serbs in retaking

Serb-controlled areas of eastern Croatia. In fact, Tudjman was welcomed to the United States for cancer treatment at Walter Reed Hospital in Washington, D.C., a few months before his death in 1999. Rumors have circulated for years that the prosecutor prepared a secret indictment against Tudjman, and former prosecutor Louise Arbour said publicly that she was working on the case. But given the time the prosecutor has taken with the Milosevic indictment, presenting the indictment concerning the Croatia war to a judge only in October 2001, the hypothesis of the existence of a secret indictment against Tudjman now seems unlikely. If there had been a secret indictment against Tudjman, there would also have been one against Milosevic. It is now clear that this was never the case. In any event, selective prosecution is rarely a valid defense, even in domestic trials.

Milosevic has also argued that NATO attacked Yugoslavia illegally in 1999. This is the same case that he made in a suit filed with the International Court of Justice in April 1999. The claim that the NATO intervention was contrary to international law is certainly not without its merits. NATO had no authorization from the United Nations Security Council to use force, and it attempted to justify the bombing attacks on Yugoslavia with an innovative and still highly questionable interpretation of the Charter of the United Nations and, more generally, of public international law. The International Court of Justice might well decide that he has a good case, if the application is ever actually heard, something that now seems unlikely given the change of regime in Belgrade.

But even if the NATO aggression argument succeeds, it can be of no help to Milosevic with respect to charges that he persecuted the Kosovar Albanians. The two issues are quite distinct, not only because the parties are not the same. Even if he were charged with crimes directed against NATO, rather than against his government's own minority population, the argument that NATO was the aggressor could not help his case. Such a defense is known to international lawyers by the Latin phrase *tu quoque,* or simply, "you did it too." Judgments issued by the ICTY make it clear that this can never be a defense to charges of grave breaches of the Geneva Conventions, violations of the laws or customs of war, genocide, or crimes against humanity.

Milosevic has also raised the issue of alleged NATO war crimes. This issue is distinct from that of the legality of the war itself. A legal war can nevertheless be waged by illegal means, just as an illegal war may be waged without violating the laws of armed conflict. At a pretrial conference in early January 2002, when Milosevic was asked to speak, he charged that NATO had attacked Yugoslavia in 1999, killing innocent people and destroying hospitals, bridges, and railways. He said NATO had sided with "Albanian terrorists."

It has come as a surprise to some U.S. politicians, but the Tribunal most certainly is empowered to prosecute NATO airmen and their commanders for war crimes committed during the Kosovo campaign. Even while the war was still raging, several respected human rights organizations urged the Tribunal to investigate the possibility that NATO had committed war crimes. The then prosecutor, Louise Arbour (from NATO member Canada), assigned the task to her legal adviser, William Fenrick. Fenrick, also a Canadian, came to the Tribunal from his post as director of law for operations and training in the Canadian Department of National Defense. Fenrick's report, released in June 2000, concluded that NATO had committed no indictable offenses.

But critics have been quick to seize upon a clause of the report that notes that the review of NATO's actions relied primarily on public documents produced by NATO and that the authors of the report "tended to assume that the NATO and NATO countries' press statements are generally reliable and that explanations have been honestly given." The Tribunal's refusal to further investigate alleged NATO war crimes has been criticized by such credible international observers as the International Committee for the Red Cross and Amnesty International. Yet whether one believes NATO violated the laws of war during the 1999 bombing campaign or not, NATO did not systematically set out to kill and torture civilians on a mass scale—the crimes for which Milosevic has been accused. The alleged NATO offenses are simply not in the same league as those for which Milosevic is charged.

Composition of the Bench

Milosevic's ultimate fate is in the hands of the Tribunal's judges, not its prosecutor. As long as the bench is impartial and the procedures are equitable, the trial of Milosevic will be considered credible. Given that the Tribunal's pool of judges who were available for the

Milosevic trial included citizens from several countries that had no stake in the Balkan conflict, the judge assigned by Chief Judge Jorda to preside over the case, Briton Richard May, represented a most unfortunate selection. Judge May is widely perceived to be the most capable trial judge at the Tribunal. The problem is that he hails from one of the NATO countries that led the 1999 intervention against Serbia. He is said to have close continuing contacts with the British Foreign Ministry. Every time Milosevic has attempted to raise the issue of NATO war crimes in Serbia, Judge May has promptly cut him off, engendering criticism about the appearance of impropriety.

Perhaps this distinguished jurist can not be expected to have recused himself from participating on the Milosevic trial, because that would have been an admission of his bias and would have subverted the credibility of the Tribunal as a whole. And yet, however fair and impartial Judge May actually turns out to be, one can certainly understand why some might believe that the "fix is in" as long as a British judge presides. Canadian law professor Michael Mandel has charged that "Milosevic has about as much chance of getting a fair trial from this court as he had of defeating NATO in an air war."

Fairness of the Procedures

Another criticism of Nuremberg that Milosevic will attempt to resurrect is the charge that the post–World War II tribunal violated due process by permitting the prosecution to base much of its case on hearsay evidence and *ex parte* (that is, prepared in the absence of the other party) affidavits. As noted in Chapter 7, in its previous cases, the ICTY has similarly permitted unfettered use of hearsay evidence by prosecution witnesses and could do the same in the Milosevic case.

Another criticism of the Nuremberg procedures was that those acquitted by the tribunal were retried and convicted in subsequent proceedings before national courts. The statute of the ICTY expressly protects defendants against double jeopardy by prohibiting national courts from retrying persons who have been tried by the International Tribunal. However, Milosevic may argue that, by permitting the Tribunal's prosecutor to appeal an acquittal, the Tribunal itself infringes the accused's interest in finality, which underlies the double jeopardy principle. Yet as discussed in Chapter 7, this expansive notion of double jeopardy is a uniquely American judicial concept. Other common law countries such as Australia, Canada, and the United Kingdom permit their prosecutors to appeal acquittals. And while it may offend U.S. sensibilities, a prosecutorial appeal is perfectly consistent with international standards of due process, as well as the practice of the courts in Serbia.

Finally, Milosevic may claim that he has been denied his right to a fair trial by adverse pretrial publicity. It is certainly not an exaggeration to say that he is widely believed to be guilty and that he has been so treated by media around the world as well as denounced publicly by prominent political figures. Within a domestic legal system, this kind of argument would have much resonance. For example, in the case of a trial by jury, judges would willingly transfer the trial, if possible, to a jurisdiction where potential jurors would be less likely to have formed an opinion about guilt or innocence. Even in the case of a bench trial (that is, by judges alone), pretrial condemnation of a defendant by political figures might lead the court to conclude that proceedings denied a right to a fair trial. International human rights tribunals have made rulings along these lines. During the trial of the two Libyan officials charged with the bombing of Pan Am 103 over Lockerbie, Scotland, in 1988, such an argument was raised. The judges rejected the claim but did not dismiss the potential validity of such an argument. They added that professional judges could generally be expected to rise above such adverse pretrial publicity.

* * * * *

In his pretrial appearances, Slobodan Milosevic adopted a trial strategy of attacking the legitimacy of the International Criminal Tribunal for the Former Yugoslavia at every opportunity rather than trying to advance a claim of genuine innocence. His refusal to "play by the rules" was blunted somewhat by the Tribunal's clever decision on the eve of trial to appoint three distinguished defense counsel to act as *amicis curiae* (friends of the court) in more ably building Milosevic's defense in court, regardless of his wishes. These lawyers have filed the motion challenging the Tribunal and formally raised the same issues in court that Milosevic himself argues.

In the end, Milosevic may be able to convince some observers that the ICTY is not quite the impartial international justice system, immune from big power influence, that its founders promised. But only the most starry-eyed of idealists could ever have imagined that power politics would play no part in the timing and targeting of the Tribunal's indictments. Despite the Nuremberg Tribunal's shortcomings, few today question the validity of its judgment, because the defendants were convicted on the strength of their own meticulously kept documents. Similarly, if the ICTY prosecutor is able to prove the case against Milosevic with compelling evidence, Milosevic will have a much harder time convincing anyone that his trial represents a denial of justice.

One of the modern myths of Nuremberg is that the German people immediately accepted the legitimacy of the tribunal. Opinion polls conducted by the United States Department of State from 1946 through 1958 indicate that a large majority of West Germans considered the Nuremberg proceedings to be nothing but a show trial, representing victor's justice rather than real justice. But two generations later, the German people speak of the Nuremberg Tribunal largely with respect, and Germany is one of the foremost advocates of the new permanent International Criminal Court. Perhaps this suggests that no matter what is the strength of the evidence, the Serb people will not immediately embrace the findings of the Yugoslavia Tribunal in the Milosevic case. The question of the Tribunal's success will await the judgment of future generations.

CHAPTER 9

The Merits of the Case

Slobodan Milosevic is now charged under three distinct indictments concerning, in chronological order, the conflicts in Croatia, Bosnia and Herzegovina, and Kosovo. The indictments alleged that he personally, or others under his command, committed one or more of the four crimes listed in the statute of the International Criminal Tribunal for the former Yugoslavia (ICTY): grave breaches of the 1949 Geneva Convention, violations of the laws or customs of war, genocide, and crimes against humanity.

Under the statute these crimes must have been committed "since 1991." The resolution of the Security Council, which created the Tribunal, clarified the meaning of this phrase as being since January 1, 1991. The crimes for which Milosevic has been indicted begin on August 1, 1991, in the case of the war in Croatia and extend to June 20, 1999 with respect to Kosovo-related allegations. There is no end date explicitly established for the jurisdiction of the Tribunal. Once again, the resolution of the Security Council assists in construing this aspect of the Tribunal's temporal scope, stating that its mandate shall continue until "a date to be determined by the Security Council upon the restoration of peace." The Security Council has not yet made such determination.

The prosecutor must also establish the existence of an armed conflict when the crimes were committed, at least for some of the offenses. As a general rule, for obvious reasons, grave breaches of the Geneva Conventions and violations of the laws or customs of war, defined in articles 2 and 3 of the ICTY statute, can be committed only in the course of an armed conflict. International law no longer insists upon the existence of an armed conflict as a condition for crimes against humanity; despite this, however, the ICTY statute imposes such a requirement in article 5. As discussed below, the prosecutor may have some difficulty proving that the sporadic confrontations between the KLA and the government forces in Kosovo rise to the level of an armed conflict as required for conviction of the charges of war crimes and crimes against humanity.

That leaves genocide, for which the statute does not require proof of an armed conflict. The *Genocide Convention* of 1948, from which article 4 of the ICTY statute derives its definition of the crime, is quite explicit in asserting that genocide may be committed in time of peace or in time of war. But at the same time, article 1 of the statute states that the Tribunal shall have the power to prosecute "serious violations of international humanitarian law." *Humanitarian law* traditionally means the law of armed conflict. Perhaps, then, the statute requires the existence of an armed conflict even in the case of a genocide indictment. Be that as it may, because there seems little doubt of the existence of an armed conflict within Bosnia and Herzegovina for all relevant parts of the indictment, the question of whether the genocide charge requires proof of armed conflict is unlikely to be the focus of the Tribunal's deliberations.

International Conflict or Civil War?

There is a related question that concerns the nature of the armed conflict. International humanitarian law distinguishes between international and noninternational armed conflict, the latter sometimes called "internal armed conflict" or "civil war." The law has always been more advanced and rigorous in the area of international armed conflict. Traditionally, states have been more willing to accept being bound by wartime legal norms when the war involved conflicts with other states. They have tended to resist the application of international law to conflicts that were essentially internal, as an encroachment on their sovereignty. Historically, states considered what they did within their own borders—suppressing a rebel group, for example—as really no one's business but their own. This is really much the same story as the growth of human rights law, which has gradually won acceptance as authority for the right of the international community to, in effect, oversee how a government treats its own people. These questions are fundamental to virtually every case coming before the ICTY. They had to be settled at the earliest stages of its operation. In 1995 the ICTY Appeals Chamber ruled that international armed conflict exists "whenever there is a resort to armed force between States." As for noninternational armed conflict, it requires "protracted armed violence between governmental authorities and organized armed groups or between such groups within a State."

Different provisions of humanitarian law will apply, depending on whether the conflict is international or noninternational. Article 2 of the statute, which punishes grave breaches of the Geneva Conventions, applies only if the conflict is international. Article 3 is much broader and covers both international and noninternational armed conflict. In practice, this has proven to be of little significance. Both the crime of "wilful killing" as a grave breach of the Geneva Conventions, punishable only in international armed conflict, and the crime of "murder" as a violation of the laws or customs of war, punishable in internal armed conflict, can be prosecuted by the Tribunal. In practice, then, anything that slips through article 2, governing international conflict, is caught by article 3. One way or another, the offender is convicted of intentional homicide. This does not mean that the trial of Milosevic may not devote considerable attention to clarifying the specifics of these questions, for ICTY judges have often done this in the past.

In contrast with the two war crimes provisions, that is, grave breaches of the Geneva Conventions and violations of the laws or customs of war, the distinction between international and noninternational armed conflict is of no significance for the prosecution of crimes against humanity. The statute is quite explicit on this point, requiring only that crimes against humanity be "committed in armed conflict, whether international or internal in character."

The prosecutor should not have too much trouble demonstrating the existence of an armed conflict, at least for the parts of the indictment dealing with Croatia and Bosnia and Herzegovina. The Tribunal has plenty of case law in which this issue has already been litigated and determined, essentially with respect to the war in Bosnia and

Herzegovina. Here the Tribunal has held in previous cases that a state of international armed conflict existed from the date Bosnia and Herzegovina proclaimed itself an independent state, on April 6, 1992. On that day it was recognized by the European Union and, the following day, by the United States. The Tribunal has resisted declaring that this issue is settled, and in the interests of the right to a fair trial it allows defendants to put these issues in dispute if they wish, despite the convincing precedents to the contrary.

It has been argued that the international character of the Bosnian war quickly disappeared with the withdrawal of regular Yugoslav troops, and that within a few weeks the conflict was purely internal. But the Tribunal rejected this approach in previous judgments, which have looked at the ongoing effective involvement of President Milosevic's Yugoslav government in the conflict until the Dayton Peace Agreement, of November 1995. Certain aspects of the wars, notably the fighting between Bosnian Croat and Bosnian Muslim militias, would be more likely to fall within the category of noninternational armed conflict or civil war (although the involvement of the Croatian government and armed forces also brought an international dimension to this part of the conflict), but this is of little concern to the Milosevic trial.

Whereas for the war in Bosnia and Herzegovina there have now been many trials and the Tribunal has clarified its outlook on these questions, the Tribunal has yet to pronounce itself on the conflict between Croatia and Yugoslavia in late 1991 and early 1992. This is the setting for the second indictment against Milosevic. When Croatia declared independence on June 25, 1991, fighting broke out between Croatian military forces on one side and the Yugoslav National Army (JNA), supported by Serb paramilitary units and the "Army of the Republic of Srpska Krajina," on the other.

But Croatia was recognized as an independent state, first by Germany and later by other members of the European Union, only at the end of 1991. In the case of Bosnia and Herzegovina, the ICTY has referred to both the declaration of independence and international recognition as evidence of the internationalization of the conflict. These dates coincide for Bosnia and Herzegovina but do not in the case of Croatia. The prosecutor has taken the position that, at the initial stages, the Croatia conflict was internal in nature. Thus, she need only establish that there was "protracted armed violence between governmental authorities and organized armed groups or between such groups within a State" as of the date when the indictment begins, August 1, 1991. Here she should have no problem. But rather than fix the internationalization of the conflict from recognition by major states, such as the European Union, which took place only months later, the prosecutor is claiming that the conflict was international as of October 8, 1991. This is the effective date of Croatia's declaration of independence. Actually, it had declared independence in June 1991, following a referendum in which the population voted overwhelmingly for independence. But on July 8, 1991, as a result of the European Union's involvement, there was an agreement that implementation of independence would be suspended for ninety days, until October 8.

There is a very real issue here that will affect whether charges of violating article 2 of the statute (grave breaches of the Geneva Conventions) can be sustained, at least for the period from August until December 1991. This is important to the prosecutor because some crucial parts of the indictment relate to events in the second half of 1991, including the siege of Vukovar and the shelling of Dubrovnik. During the second half of 1991 it can be argued that the war was only internal, given that Croatia had not yet been recognized by the European Union or the United States nor yet been admitted to the United Nations or the Organization for Security and Cooperation in Europe. Indeed, by the beginning of 1992, when recognition by the European Union would seem to confirm the international identity of Croatia and thus the internationalization of the conflict, there was an effective ceasefire between Serbian and Croatian forces. Milosevic can succeed in obtaining dismissal of some of the charges, particularly those alleging grave breaches of the Geneva Conventions, if he can raise a reasonable doubt that the conflict in Croatia was international. But this will not get him off the hook with respect to violations of article 3 of the statute, because these can be committed in internal armed conflict.

Kosovo: A Purely Internal Conflict

With respect to the Kosovo indictment, the prosecutor is not relying on the assertion that there was a state of international armed conflict, though of course there was. On the eve of the NATO bombing campaign, Yugoslavia proclaimed a state of imminent threat of war on March 23, 1999, and a state of war on March 24, 1999, so there can be no serious argument by Milosevic that there was no international armed conflict for much of the period covered by the indictment. But that is not the issue. The prosecutor also needs to establish that there was a noninternational, or internal, armed conflict in Kosovo during the first six months of 1999.

There was of course no declaration of independence or recognition of Kosovo's independence, as in the cases of Croatia and Bosnia and Herzegovina. Kosovo has never been anything but an administrative district of Yugoslavia, although since the end of the conflict in 1999 it has enjoyed a form of *de facto* autonomy under a United Nations regime. Undoubtedly the conflict became internationalized with the NATO bombing campaign, which started in late March 1999 and continued until June of that year. But while this may be relevant to eventual charges against either Milosevic and his soldiers or the NATO forces, with respect to what they did to each other, it is not really germane to the issue of what Milosevic did to citizens of Yugoslavia within its own sovereign borders, which included Kosovo.

The prosecutor is treating the Kosovo conflict that took place in the first half of 1999 as an internal or noninternational one. No charges have been made with respect to article 2 of the statute, which governs grave breaches of the Geneva Conventions and applies only to international armed conflict. As with the first months of the Croatian conflict, then, the prosecutor will have to prove that in the first six months of 1999 there existed "protracted armed violence between governmental authorities and organized armed groups or between such groups within a State."

There can be no doubt that by the mid-1990s, there existed in Kosovo an organized group known as the *Ushtria Çlirimtare e Kosovës* (UÇK) or, in English, the Kosovo Liberation Army (KLA). It advocated a campaign of armed insurgency against and violent resistance to the Serbian authorities, launching attacks principally against Serbian police forces. The Serbian police forces met these attacks with force, as one would expect.

There is a fuzzy line in international law at the low end of internal or noninternational armed conflict. At what point does a conflict with organized armed groups cease to meet the threshold of "protracted armed violence" and become mere "situations of internal disturbances and tensions, such as riots, isolated and sporadic acts of violence or other acts of a similar nature," the expression used by international law treaties to define situations not covered by the laws of armed conflict? This is the issue that the prosecutor will have to address. Because of the wording of the statute and its theoretically unnecessary requirement that crimes against humanity be committed in connection with armed conflict, the ICTY simply lacks jurisdiction to prosecute Milosevic if the prosecutor fails to establish that there was a state of armed conflict. There is a possible exception to this in the case of genocide, but it is of no practical significance because Milosevic is not charged with genocide in the case of the Kosovo conflict. Thus, the prosecutor's allegation that Milosevic "planned, instigated, ordered, committed or otherwise aided and abetted in a deliberate and widespread or systematic campaign of terror and violence directed at Kosovo Albanian civilians living in Kosovo" fails if she cannot demonstrate that these acts were committed as part of an armed conflict.

One possible approach for the prosecutor would be to claim a state of armed conflict has existed more or less continuously in the territory of the former Yugoslavia since mid-1991. The difficulty here is that there was a period of relative calm throughout the territory following the Dayton Peace Agreement of December 1995. By 1998 internal tensions in Kosovo had escalated to the point that there were major refugee flows. In March 1998 the United Nations Security Council condemned "the use of excessive force by Serbian police forces against civilians and peaceful demonstrators in Kosovo" and imposed an arms embargo. Six months later, the council declared that "the deterioration of the situation in Kosovo, Federal Republic of Yugoslavia, constitutes a threat to peace and security in the region." Yet in an attempt to defuse the escalating conflict, the Organization for Security and Cooperation in Europe (OSCE) sent many hundreds of unarmed observers (the Kosovo indictment refers to "scores") to verify the situation. The OSCE monitors found much evidence of persecution by the Serb authorities, including the notorious massacre at Racak in January 1999. But is it really conceivable that the OSCE would have considered such a mission in the midst of an armed conflict? Undoubtedly, the prosecutor will bring some of the OSCE verifiers to testify about the nature and level of the violence in order to convince the Tribunal that there was indeed a situation of internal armed conflict.

Milosevic could argue that the mere presence of OSCE verifiers tends to prove there was no armed conflict in Kosovo in early 1999. However, his initial forays at cross-examination suggest he does not plan to make this argument. Perhaps he is not even aware of it, or he does not take it seriously. He seems to take the view that there was indeed a serious rebel movement within Kosovo, capable of sustained armed engagements. He is presenting this as justification for the robust response of the Yugoslav armed forces and police.

While the specific facts of the indictments must all be proven by the prosecutor, there can be little doubt that terrible violence and atrocities took place, with some interludes of relative calm, in the territory of the former Yugoslavia between mid-1991 and June 1999. This is common knowledge and is unlikely to be strongly contested by the defense, though that does not of course obviate the prosecutor's obligation to introduce evidence to prove all relevant facts. It is possible for the defense to make admissions, in effect conceding the truth of certain facts and relieving the prosecution of the need to lead evidence. A good defense lawyer will willingly cooperate in such a process as a general rule, and judges will prevail upon counsel's professional reputation in order to encourage such a process. Defense lawyers tend toward such a cooperative posture because they must return again and again to the same court; it is their professional forum. But this is very unlikely to happen in the Milosevic trial. By refusing to retain counsel, he has eliminated any chance that the judges can exert pressure to cooperate and thereby expedite the trial. And Milosevic himself is unlikely to concede anything.

For the prosecutor, much of this will be more of a chore than anything else, precisely because many of the facts are not really in dispute. The heart of the issue is not whether killing, destruction of property and similar violent acts took place, but whether Milosevic can be associated with them as a principal offender or as some form of accomplice.

"Joint Criminal Enterprise"

The ICTY statute allows for trial and conviction of a "person who planned, instigated, ordered, committed or otherwise aided and abetted in the planning, preparation or execution" of grave breaches, violations of the laws or customs of war, genocide or crimes against humanity. The prosecutor makes it quite clear in the indictments that Milosevic did not physically commit the murders and other acts with which he is charged. The prosecutor has taken the position that Milosevic "committed" the crimes in that he participated in "a joint criminal enterprise as a co-perpetrator." This concept of "joint criminal enterprise" is a relatively new idea. Although it appears in the 2001 indictments of Milosevic prepared by Carla Del Ponte, it was nowhere mentioned in the May 1999 indictment of Milosevic that was signed by her predecessor, Louise Arbour. The prosecutor seems to have taken the idea from the judges of the Appeals Chamber, who, in a July 1999 ruling upholding the conviction of Dusko Tadic, discussed the concept of "joint criminal enterprise" at some length. They appear to have adapted the idea from some of the post–World War II judgments rendered by British and other military tribunals.

There is a "joint criminal enterprise" when two or more persons have a form of agreement, even one that is only inferred and of which there is no direct proof, to carry out a crime. An individual participates in the "joint criminal enterprise" when he or she actually participates physically in committing the crime or is present when the crime is committed and assists or encourages another to commit the crime. But more important for the Milosevic case, such a "joint criminal enterprise" also exists when an individual acts in furtherance of a particular system in which the crime is committed by reason of the person's position of authority. An individual who participates in such a joint criminal enterprise is guilty of the crime that is committed— that is, for the acts that others commit in pursuance of the criminal enterprise—regardless of the part he or she plays.

The purpose of the joint criminal enterprise in which Milosevic participated according to the three indictments, was what is commonly known as "ethnic cleansing." In the case of Croatia, this enterprise sought the forcible removal of the Croat and other non-Serb populations from the eastern part of Croatia (principally, the Krajina and Western Slavonia) and the Dubrovnik area, all with a view to incorporating the "cleansed" territory in a new Serb-dominated state. With respect to Bosnia and Herzegovina, the principal targets for forcible and permanent removal were Bosnian Muslims and Bosnian Croats. Similar allegations are made concerning the Kosovo

Albanians. The objective was the expulsion of a substantial portion of the Kosovo Albanian population from the territory of Kosovo in an effort to ensure continued Serbian control over the troubled province.

There appear to be two phases in the prosecutor's analysis of this joint criminal enterprise. The first began prior to August 1991 and was targeted at the ethnic cleansing in Croatia and, somewhat later, Bosnia and Herzegovina. Its members included Zeljko Raznatovic (aka "Arkan"), Borisav Jovic, Branko Kostic, Veljko Kadijevic, Blagoje Adzic, Milan Martic, Jovica Stanisic, Franko Simatovic (aka "Franki"), Radovan Stojicic (aka "Badza"), and Vojislav Seselj. Within Bosnia and Herzegovina, Bosnian Serb leaders Radovan Karadzic, Momcilo Krajisnik, Biljana Plavsic, and General Ratko Mladic are also alleged to have participated. The second phase dates from 1998 and includes Milan Milutinovic, Nikola Sainovic, Dragoljub Ojdanic and Vlajka Stojiljkovic. These four are also indicted together with Milosevic.

The indictments note that Milosevic was the "dominant political figure" in Serbia from 1987 to late 2000. He is said to have controlled "all facets of the Serbian government, including the police and other state security services." Moreover, Milosevic held the leading position in the SDS party, and at relevant times he effectively controlled the federal presidency of the Socialist Federal Republic of Yugoslavia (and its successor, the Federal Republic of Yugoslavia), the Serbian Ministry of Internal Affairs, the Yugoslav National Army (later known as the Armed Forces of the Federal Republic of Yugoslavia), the Serb-run Territorial Defense staff, and various Serb volunteer groups and irregular militias, such as "Seselj's men," "Martic's Police," "Arkan's Tigers," and the "White Eagles."

In effect, then, because of the dominant position held by Milosevic throughout the political and military structures of what remained of Yugoslavia following the secession of Slovenia, Croatia, Macedonia, and Bosnia and Herzegovina, essentially all criminal acts carried out by official or quasi-official forces can be laid at his door. This is conditional, of course, on proving the existence of a "common enterprise" to ethnically cleanse the territories in question. Nothing in the indictment alleges a meeting or anything comparable where the ethnic cleansing was organized, along the lines of the infamous Wannsee Conference held in Nazi Germany in January 1942. But proof of some agreement or conspiracy to commit ethnic cleansing, either in the form of documents or actual eyewitness testimony, would make the prosecutor's case a strong one indeed.

But this seems unlikely. Nazi Germany, which was arguably more organized than the various components of the Serbian government, left an enormous documentary record of its atrocities. Admittedly, historians continue to argue about how structured the decision to carry out the "final solution" at Auschwitz-Birkenau and the other extermination camps really was and how many of the senior Nazis were actually involved in it and aware of its scope. (This is not the same argument as the spurious, provocative, and illegitimate attempts of some pseudo-historians to challenge whether genocide actually took place.) Despite these problems, however, there can be no doubt that there was a joint criminal enterprise in Nazi Germany to exterminate the Jews of Europe. Even though Hitler did not attend the Wannsee Conference, the conclusion that he masterminded the genocide is a reasonable deduction from the context and from circumstantial evidence of which there can really be no doubt. Likewise in the Yugoslav context, if the prosecutor can succeed in demonstrating the existence of a joint criminal enterprise to ethnically cleanse Kosovo and parts of Croatia and Bosnia and Herzegovina, that Milosevic was its chief architect would seem to be the only logical conclusion.

Or Was He Just Asleep at the Controls?

Should the prosecutor fail to convince the judges of the existence of a joint criminal enterprise, she has a second line of attack. She can fall back on a second form of criminal responsibility known as "command or superior responsibility." On this basis, she need only show that the accused was a commander or superior and that persons under his supervision committed the crimes alleged in the indictment. In reality, the accused is not charged with knowingly participating in the crime but merely with being negligent about its commission, somewhat in the same way that the manager of an ecologically unfriendly factory might be charged with damaging the local environment. The manager can escape liability only by proving he or she acted with due diligence to prevent the harm done to the environment. In the case of war crimes, the commander or superior can escape liability only by producing evidence to suggest he or she took "the necessary and reasonable measures" to prevent the crimes taking place.

The Tribunal may never get to this issue because, should it conclude Milosevic is responsible as part of a "joint criminal enterprise," it may not need to examine the other approach to criminal liability. But in the general scheme of things, it should be easier to convict Milosevic on the basis of command or superior responsibility, because all that needs to be proven is that the crime in question was committed by a subordinate and that Milosevic was actually the person in effective command. He can of course argue that there was no real line of command with him at the top or that he was simply too remote because there were too many links in the chain of command. That argument may work to the extent that specific acts appear to be isolated. The more they seem widespread or systematic, the less plausible is the argument that Milosevic should not have been aware of their commission.

Whether the prosecutor operates on the basis of "joint criminal enterprise" or "command responsibility," she must in any event establish that the underlying crimes took place. She will have to prove that killings or other prohibited acts were committed—by others—and that these rose to the level of grave breaches of the Geneva Conventions, violations of the laws or customs of war, genocide, or crimes against humanity. Under "joint criminal enterprise," she must prove there was some common purpose, namely, the ethnic cleansing of the regions in question, and that Milosevic played a material part in the carrying out of such purpose. Under "command responsibility," she need only prove that the acts were committed by persons subordinate to Milosevic, leaving him to answer this with proof that he tried reasonably to prevent the acts taking place or to punish the perpetrators.

Many of the underlying facts involved in proving command or superior responsibility will not be difficult to establish. Some of this involves merely demonstrating the legal structure of the defense forces and related bodies. For example, there is likely to be little difficulty with the assertion that Milosevic was, as president of the Federal Republic of Yugoslavia, the president of the Supreme Defense Council of the Federal Republic of Yugoslavia and the supreme commander of the armed forces. According to the Law on Defense of the Federal Republic of Yugoslavia, the supreme commander of the armed forces also exercised command authority over republican police units subordinated to the armed forces during a state of imminent threat of war or a state of war. Milosevic's paramount role within the government can also be presumed because of his participation in various international negotiations during the crisis, from those held at The Hague in 1991 to the Dayton meetings in late 1995.

A considerably greater challenge will be proving the scope of the informal or *de facto* powers that Milosevic exercised within the Serb military, paramilitary, and police establishment. The ICTY has already recognized in previous judgments that command or superior responsibility can exist even when the superior-subordinate relationship is only *de facto*, not based on a legal obligation. In support, it has referred to World War II cases that seem to make the same point.

With respect to Milosevic, the prosecutor claims such *de facto* control includes various institutions nominally under the authority of Serbia and the autonomous provinces, such as the Serbian police force. In effect, this claim means proving that Yugoslavia was a dictatorship and that Milosevic was the dictator, an argument that may wash at a journalistic level but is far from easy to make in a court of law. But in effect, the prosecutor is claiming that from 1988 until his downfall in 2000, Milosevic exercised such control over virtually all institutions, not only military ones, within the Socialist Federal Republic of Yugoslavia, then the Federal Republic of Yugoslavia, and in Serbia, Montenegro, Kosovo, and Vojvodina. In some cases the prosecutor says Milosevic exercised his *de facto* control because he had "effective control" over other individuals. These people acted as his "primary agents" and they are alleged to have "acted without dissension to execute Slobodan Milosevic's policies."

Sometimes the prosecutor seems to be hedging her position, claiming that Milosevic either exercised effective control or "substantially influenced individuals and organizations." This appears to be the case, for example, with the Bosnian Serb armed forces, or VRS. It would seem implausible, however, that the Tribunal will extend the concept of command responsibility to accused persons who only "substantially influence" others. The difficulty for the prosecutor will be particularly acute with respect to Bosnia and Herzegovina, where, owing to the independent Bosnian Serb institutions and military forces, the chain of command becomes muddied at best.

The prosecutor contends that, pursuant to his authority both in law and *de facto*, Milosevic is criminally responsible for any grave breaches, violations of the laws or customs of war, genocide, or crimes against humanity that were committed by members of the armed forces of the Federal Republic of Yugoslavia and Serbia, including those of the Serbian ministry of interior, military-territorial units, civil defense units, and other armed groups operating under their authority or with their knowledge. With respect to Bosnia and Herzegovina, however, the prosecutor is not trying to argue that Milosevic also exercised control over the various military units of the Bosnian Serbs. Nor has she claimed that the Bosnian Serb leaders, Karadzic, Mladic, and others, were his subordinates or even that he exercised substantial influence over them.

As a commander, Milosevic had an obligation to remain informed about the activities of his subordinates. But while, in a strictly military sense or based on *de facto* authority, it might be argued that there was a chain of command stretching from Milosevic down to the soldier or militia member at the lowest level, it seems to stretch the doctrine of command responsibility to attempt to hold the head of State, even one alleged to be a dictator, responsible for every act or omission committed by those under his authority. To take one example: in the absence of evidence of some plan or order to commit such crimes, is it reasonable to hold Milosevic responsible for every rape or sexual assault committed by Yugoslav troops during the conflict? If he is to be held responsible for such acts, it seems only fair to insist on evidence that this was actually a policy and that he either ordered their commission or implicitly authorized them. If this were true, then it would appear to be more a case of "joint criminal enterprise" than of "command responsibility." In other words, at the level of the supreme commander, these concepts seem almost to merge together.

Should he not succeed in breaking the chain of command, the burden of proof shifts to Milosevic, who may then attempt to establish that he took necessary and reasonable measures to prevent such acts. Silence is not enough. Without a credible explanation, he is likely to be convicted.

But Milosevic may also attempt to challenge the law on command or superior responsibility. He has at least one avenue of attack. It has yet to be decided whether it is even possible to commit genocide by means of command responsibility. The Genocide Convention of 1948 requires that the prosecution establish a particularly high level of intent—the accused must intend to physically destroy the ethnic group, in whole or in part—and the Tribunal has not yet resolved how such a crime can be committed by mere negligent supervision of subordinates. This intriguing argument may work for the genocide indictment but is of less interest with respect to the other charges.

Ethnic Cleansing

Ethnic cleansing is not mentioned anywhere in the ICTY statute, and it has never been authoritatively defined in international law. The expression *ethnic cleansing* first appeared in 1981 in Yugoslav media accounts of the establishment of "ethnically clean territories" in Kosovo. The term entered the international vocabulary in 1992 and was used to describe policies being pursued by the various parties to the Yugoslav conflict aimed at creating ethnically homogeneous territories. There have been a number of attempts at definition. According to the UN Security Council's Commission of Experts on violations of humanitarian law during the Yugoslav war, "the expression 'ethnic cleansing' is relatively new. Considered in the context of the conflicts in the former Yugoslavia, 'ethnic cleansing' means rendering an area ethnically homogeneous by using force or intimidation to remove persons of given groups from the area."

Milosevic is charged with "ethnic cleansing" by carrying out specific war crimes and crimes against humanity, such as murder, persecution, and deportation. Typically, according to the indictment, the various Serb forces would take control of a town or village and order the inhabitants to surrender any weapons. Then the civilians would be attacked, even those who had complied with the order to disarm. Such attacks, says the prosecutor, were intended to compel the population to flee. Any who remained would be rounded up and transported out of the region. Often a series of restrictive and discriminatory measures, and even a campaign of terror, would be used to incite people to leave. The indictments also make very precise references to extermination and murder of thousands of Croatians, Bosnian Muslims, and Kosovo Albanians during the three wars, in Croatia, Bosnia and Herzegovina, and Kosovo. Specific victims are named in annexes to the indictments. These very brutal acts of violence were accompanied by an underlying climate of persecution, involving racial slurs; insults; physical and psychological mistreatment based on racial, religious, and political identification;

restriction of freedom of movement; removal from positions of authority in local government institutions and the police; dismissal from jobs; arbitrary searches of homes; denial of the right to judicial process; and denial of the right of equal access to public services, including proper medical care.

Thousands of Croatians and Muslims were imprisoned in camps within Croatia and, later, Bosnia and Herzegovina. Some of the camps became infamous in international media when they were exposed by journalists like Penny Marshall, Roy Gutman, and Ed Vulliamy. Photos of their emaciated inmates recalled images of Dachau and Auschwitz. The indictment of Milosevic alleges that this was part of the overall scheme of ethnic cleansing and that it may even have risen to the level of genocide. The living conditions in these detention facilities were brutal and characterized by inhumane treatment, overcrowding, starvation, inadequate medical care, and constant physical and psychological assault, including mock executions, torture, beatings, and sexual assault. While in detention, those imprisoned were also enlisted as prolonged and frequent forced labor for the Serb forces, such as digging graves or trenches and loading ammunition.

The ethnic cleansing also involved extensive crimes against property. Destruction of homes and other public and private property would render towns and villages uninhabitable and discourage the persecuted populations from ever returning. Attacks on cultural institutions, historic monuments, and sacred sites would remove any traces of the original ethnic groups that had inhabited the region. The Croatia indictment focuses in particular on the military campaign directed at the historic Croatian city of Dubrovnik, including its Old Town, which is a UNESCO World Cultural Heritage Site. From October to December 1991 Serb forces attacked Dubrovnik to achieve the forcible removal of its non-Serb population. The ultimate goal was to detach the area, located at the southern tip of Croatia, and annex it to Montenegro. The attack included an unlawful shelling campaign conducted from military positions on land and on sea. It is alleged that some forty-three Croat civilians, all of them named as victims in the indictment, were killed during these attacks. The shelling also resulted in the destruction of homes; religious, historical, and cultural buildings; and other civilian public or private buildings. Many of the buildings that were attacked had been identified with the protective symbols of the 1954 Hague Convention on the Protection of Cultural Property in the Event of Armed Conflict. There were no military targets either on or within the walls of the Old Town, and there could be no conceivable military advantage from such attacks.

The indictments focus on several of the most notorious atrocities committed during the three wars. The first of the large-scale mass executions occurred in the hospital in Vukovar, in Eastern Slavonia, virtually on the border with Serbia. Serb forces took over the town in November 1991, following a siege. During the encirclement, the city was largely destroyed by shelling, and hundreds of civilians were killed. Serb forces are alleged to have taken 250 patients from the municipal hospital, removing them to a military barracks and then to a farm. There, the Serb forces are charged with beating and torturing their prisoners before transporting them to an execution site where they were shot and buried in a mass grave.

The Bosnian indictment charges Milosevic with responsibility for a wide range of crimes, including sniping and shelling attacks during the siege of Sarajevo. Over forty-four months, the Sarajevo Romanija Corps of the Bosnian Serb forces, which were ostensibly under the effective control of Radovan Karadzic and General Ratko Mladic, launched an extensive shelling and sniping attack on Sarajevo, mostly from positions in the hills surrounding the city. Civilians were either specifically targeted or the subject of reckless fire into areas where they were known to be living. Civilian victims of the sniping were killed while tending vegetable plots, queuing for bread or water, attending funerals, shopping in markets, riding on trams, and gathering wood.

The prosecution's case will call on the Tribunal to address some of the lingering controversies concerning specific incidents that took place in the former Yugoslavia, some of which have occasioned mutual recriminations and accusations. By addressing these matters the ICTY will fulfill part of its overall responsibility to provide historical clarification. For example, Milosevic is accused of responsibility for what is probably the most notorious of the attacks on Sarajevo. On February 5, 1994, a 120-millimeter mortar shell hit a crowded open-air market called "Markale," situated in a civilian area of Old Town Sarajevo. Sixty-six people were killed, and over 140 people were wounded, including three children under the age of fifteen. The prosecutor alleges that the origin of fire was territory held by the Bosnian Serb military. Proving this will be a complicated endeavor for the prosecutor. First, she must demonstrate, presumably using military experts, that the trajectory of the mortar shell leads inexorably to the conclusion that it came from Bosnian Serb positions. Then, she must also establish that the Bosnian Serb forces—Karadzic and Mladic—were part of the "criminal enterprise" at whose head stood Milosevic.

Another notorious atrocity, but one for which the facts also remain highly contested to this day, is the mass killing in Racak, a town about twenty miles south of Kosovo's capital, Pristina, that took place on or about January 15, 1999. Racak had been subject to vicious ethnic cleansing of its mainly Kosovo Albanian population during 1998, and by the beginning of 1999 only 350 of its original 2,000 inhabitants were still living there. The Kosovo Albanian guerrillas known as the UÇK had established a base near the town's power plant. From January 12 to 15, 1999, both guerrilla and Yugoslav government forces intensified their activities. The village was shelled by forces of the Federal Republic of Yugoslavia and Serbia, who then entered Racak and began conducting house to house searches. Monitors from the Organization for Security and Cooperation in Europe (OSCE) later stumbled upon the massacre site, where they found approximately forty-five bodies. Both sides have charged the other with responsibility for the killings. The Trial Chamber of the ICTY must settle this matter.

The Crime of Crimes: Genocide

The most serious of the general accusations against Milosevic is that he committed genocide. Whether genocide actually took place in Yugoslavia has been the subject of much debate. In 1993 Bosnia and Herzegovina sued Yugoslavia before the International Court of Justice for violating the 1948 Genocide Convention. However, the court has yet to make a definitive ruling. Legally, the issue is whether the forced expulsion or "cleansing" of an ethnic group, using terror tactics and various forms of persecution, amounts to "the intentional destruction of the group in whole or in part," the recognized international legal definition of genocide.

Neither the Kosovo nor the Croatia indictment contains counts for the crime of genocide. Only the third and last of the indictments, dealing with Bosnia and Herzegovina, makes this charge. There is a general allegation that the persecution of Muslims and Croats in the Bosnian concentration camps was genocidal in nature because it involved killing, serious bodily and mental harm, and the imposition of material conditions calculated to destroy the group. The prosecutor also charges that Serb forces targeted educated and leading members of the Bosnian Muslim and Bosnian Croat minorities for execution, often in accordance with prepared lists. Here the theory is that destruction of the elite or leadership of an ethnic group strikes at its very existence and thus can constitute genocide. Both of these issues raise important questions about the definition of genocide on which the ICTY Appeals Chamber has yet to make a definitive ruling. The handful of cases decided to date send contradictory signals on these matters.

The heart of the genocide charge, however, involves the alleged involvement of Milosevic in the Srebrenica massacre. Over the course of a few days in July 1995, some seven thousand to eight thousand Muslim men and boys of military age were summarily executed. Prior to the killings, the women, children, and the elderly were forcibly evacuated from the region. In the *Krstic* case, decided in early August 2001, the ICTY ruled that the Srebrenica killings amounted to genocide. This was the first conviction for genocide by the ICTY. The judges in the *Krstic* case pointed their accusing fingers directly at the Bosnian Serb military leader General Ratko Mladic, who was not himself indicted in that trial, as the massacre's architect. Interestingly, however, they made no reference to any alleged complicity of Slobodan Milosevic. But if Milosevic is part, as the prosecutor charges, of a joint criminal enterprise of which Mladic is a central member, then complicity in the Srebrenica atrocity should extend to the door of the former Yugoslav president, as well.

Proof beyond a Reasonable Doubt

The prosecution must prove its case "beyond a reasonable doubt." Milosevic is entitled to the benefit of the doubt as to whether the offense has been proved. In a 1998 judgment, the ICTY held: "A reasonable doubt is a doubt which the particular jury entertain in the circumstances. Jurymen themselves set the standard of what is reasonable in the circumstances. It is that ability which is attributed to them which is one of the virtues of our mode of trial: to their task of deciding facts they bring to bear their experience and judgment." Reasonable doubt is thus a somewhat enigmatic concept. Courts have often described a "reasonable" doubt as a doubt that is founded in reason. It does not mean "any doubt," "beyond a shadow of a doubt," "absolute certainty," or "moral certainty." Nor, on the other end of the scale, does it imply "an actual substantive doubt" or "such doubt as would give rise to a grave uncertainty." The reasonable doubt standard has to be considered based on the evidence as a whole. It does not mean that there must be no reasonable doubt about every single aspect of the evidence.

Before Milosevic has even said a word in his defense, the prosecutor must establish that Milosevic was responsible, either as a member of a "joint criminal enterprise" or through negligent supervision of those under his command, for all of the basic elements of the crimes with which he is charged. At the close of the prosecution's evidence, prior to presentation of the case for the defense, Milosevic may challenge the sufficiency of the prosecution's case and ask that it be dismissed. On more than one occasion, ICTY judges have summarily ended trials at this stage because of the prosecutor's failure to present enough evidence. This is simply a corollary of the principle of the presumption of innocence, which is explicitly affirmed in article 21 of the ICTY statute.

Slobodan Milosevic benefits from the right of an accused not to be compelled to testify against himself or to confess guilt. He is not required even to make a case for the defense, and may simply challenge the sufficiency of the prosecution's evidence. It is impossible to predict whether the stubborn and belligerent approach he has taken during the trial's initial phase will carry over into the defense phase of the trial.

In theory, at any rate, Milosevic was required to submit a brief to the pretrial judge, setting out the factual and legal issues that he intends to raise and providing a general description of the nature of his defense and the matters in the prosecutor's submissions with which he takes issue. The pretrial judge was empowered to order him to submit a list of witnesses with a summary of the facts on which they will testify, as well as a list of any material exhibits. Obviously, the uncooperative defendant who consistently refused to recognize the

legitimacy of the Tribunal did not respect these procedural requirements. During the trial, should Milosevic attempt to make a defense,
the judges will have to decide whether his refusal to cooperate at the
pretrial stage meant that he forfeited the possibility of testifying himself, or producing witnesses and documents, or even arguing the
admissibility of certain defenses. In the interests of ensuring a fair trial
for the accused and ensuring that any conviction leave no doubt as to
innocence, they are unlikely to impose such a draconian provision.

Although the prosecutor is required to provide proof beyond a
reasonable doubt, Milosevic need only raise a reasonable doubt in
order to demolish one or more elements of the evidence against him.
For example, he is charged with responsibility for the mortar shell
that hit the market in Old Town Sarajevo on February 5, 1994, killing
sixty-six civilians, because it was allegedly fired by Bosnian Serb
forces. There have been many lingering questions about the trajectory of the shell and its precise origin. Any *reasonable* doubt that
Milosevic can raise about the facts of the atrocity will be sufficient to
eliminate this issue from the case against him.

At the most basic level, the prosecution's case depends on very
specific factual allegations, and all of these can be attacked by the
defense. Yet while there may be an arguable case with respect to the
attack on the Sarajevo market or to a precise charge dealing with
civilian casualties in Sarajevo's "sniper alley," most of the factual allegations are unlikely to be contested. It seems highly unlikely, especially given the very primitive nature of Milosevic's challenge to the
indictments, that he will attempt to investigate and contest such
detailed factual allegations. The prosecutor has never alleged that
Milosevic knew the shell would be fired or that he gave an order to
attack the market, only that this was one of the more horrendous
episodes in an overall campaign of terror in which he had a part. In
other words, if the prosecutor can make a convincing case on these
points, the factual allegations will stand.

A Strategy for the Defence

The main factual issue that Milosevic is likely to contest, and about
which he may have personal knowledge and, perhaps, serious arguments to submit, relates to his command and control. Presumably he
will deny the existence of the "joint criminal enterprise" that the pros-

ecutor claims he masterminded and that is the core of her case. Milosevic may testify himself on this point and call witnesses and other evidence. He may describe meetings with his subordinates and attempt to characterize his relationship with the Bosnian Serb leadership in such a way as to suggest that he was not an accomplice to some or all of the atrocities. Nobody can dispute that he knows the situation better than anyone. But will the judges believe him? The real test may come when he is cross-examined by the prosecutor. This is the price he must pay if he intends to testify in his own defense.

A verbal duel between the prosecutor and Milosevic will surely be one of the great and dramatic moments in international criminal justice. It will recall the famous cross-examination of the Nazi leader Hermann Göring at Nuremberg. Woefully underestimated by the prosecutor, Robert Jackson, who found himself out of practice after many years on the bench, Göring scored point after point and never gave up the advantage to his attackers. As Judge Birkett wrote in his account of the trial, "The cross examination had not proceeded more than ten minutes before it was seen that [Göring] was the complete master of Mr. Justice Jackson." Ultimately this proved to be of little help in the trial as a whole, because Göring refused to meet the prosecution's case head on. Convinced that he would lose a staged trial, Göring merely exploited the occasion for propaganda purposes. Milosevic's behavior in court during the pretrial phase suggests he may well be toying with the same kind of strategy. But no prosecutor should underestimate his abilities or count on winning the case through artful questioning of the man.

To ensure a fair trial, the judges are unlikely to leave the defense to Milosevic himself. Already, they have named a team of distinguished international criminal lawyers as *amici curiae,* assigning them the responsibility to raise legal and factual issues and to provide an alternative to the prosecutor's version of the facts. The *amici curiae* are entitled even to question and cross-examine witnesses. Moreover, the judges also have the power to summon witnesses on their own initiative or to compel the production of material evidence. Whether they will actually do this remains to be seen and may in fact depend upon how impressed they are with the quality of the prosecution's case.

Finally, in his rather laconic comments before the Tribunal during the pretrial phase, Milosevic has also suggested that he brought peace to Yugoslavia. It is of course quite true that he was the principal negotiator for Yugoslavia, and that he represented the Bosnian Serbs as well, during the Dayton peace conference in late 1995. The problem with Milosevic's argument is that it is like comparing apples and oranges. Milosevic's role in bringing the conflict to an end is simply not germane to the issue of whether atrocities were committed while it was being carried out. The issues are totally distinct.

Yet if Milosevic succeeds in making the point that he was the peacemaker, this may help his case with respect to the relationship he had with the Bosnian Serb leadership. Radovan Karadzic, his counterpart among the Bosnian Serbs, had already been indicted by the ICTY prior to the November 1995 Dayton Peace Agreement, and principally for this reason he refused to travel to the United States for the negotiations. The claim that Milosevic was an accomplice in such atrocities as the Srebrenica massacre rests to a large extent on convincing the judges of a close, integrated relationship between the Belgrade regime and its associates in Bosnia and Herzegovina. Underlying the argument that Milosevic brought peace to Bosnia and Herzegovina may sit claims that, despite appearances, in reality he had a difficult and tense relationship with the Bosnian Serb leaders.

Many of the factual and legal issues likely to arise during the trial have already been addressed by the ICTY in one form or another in previous judgments. For example, the fact situation of the Srebrenica massacre seems unlikely to be reassessed by the judges during the Milosevic trial, for it was examined in detail during the *Krstic* trial, which ended in a conviction in August 2001. Presumably, the prosecutor will present essentially the same evidence during the trial of Milosevic. But major issues may arise in assessing whether the Srebrenica massacre should be categorized as genocide rather than crimes against humanity. In the *Krstic* case, three judges found that the summary execution of military-age men and boys within a precise geographic region constituted the destruction of a significant portion of an ethnic group and could therefore be described as genocide. A ruling in the *Sikirica* case one month later appears to go in the other direction. The *Krstic* interpretation of genocide is a novel one, without much support in legal literature, and might well be viewed differently by the judges in the Milosevic trial. Besides Srebrenica, the genocide accusations against Milosevic are based more broadly on the claim that the range of atrocities associated with ethnic cleansing, including the persecutions of Croats and Muslims in concentration camps, amounted to genocide. Twice now this claim has failed before the ICTY in other cases.

Retroactive Prosecution?

Defendants have not infrequently challenged indictments on the ground that they represent a form of retroactive prosecution. Judges of the ICTY have then been forced to consider whether the statute's provisions were already recognized as part of customary international law at the time of their commission. The terms of the ICTY statute are themselves often rather vague, leaving room for various interpretations. For example, the crime of rape, set out in article 5 as a crime against humanity, means different things in different legal systems. Out of fairness to the accused, the Tribunal has looked at customary law as well as the law previously in force in Yugoslavia to avoid any claim of punishing an accused for something that was not clearly recognized as criminal at the time of its commission.

Most of the specific crimes with which Milosevic is charged leave little room for such an argument. For example, he cannot contest the legitimacy of prosecution for grave breaches of the Geneva Conventions. The law has been relatively clear on this since 1949, when the Conventions were adopted, and they have been incorporated into the domestic law of many countries, including the former Yugoslavia. There is somewhat more room for him to raise the issue with respect to violations of the laws or customs of war, except that earlier decisions of the Tribunal have already given this question considerable attention.

Ultimately, the defense of Milosevic—should he even present one—will stand or fail on proof that there really was a joint criminal enterprise to effect ethnic cleansing by means of various forms of terror. The evidence is likely to be largely circumstantial, and while this does not make prosecution impossible, it leaves the case exposed to attack for not meeting the standard of reasonable doubt. The judges may consider that, though he was responsible for the conduct of international and internal conflicts in Croatia, Bosnia and Herzegovina, and finally, in Kosovo, the specific atrocities were carried out by low-level officials who were simply too remote from Milosevic to justify holding him personally responsible for their conduct.

CHAPTER 10

The Outcome

If Slobodan Milosevic is convicted, the International Criminal Tribunal for the Former Yugoslavia (ICTY) will sentence him to a term of imprisonment. The Tribunal does not have its own prison, aside from the remand center in Scheveningen where prisoners are held prior to and during their trials. But actual sentences are served in national prisons of countries with which the Tribunal has negotiated an arrangement. They are subject to the national laws applicable to that country's prisons, although a degree of supervision continues to be exercised by the Tribunal's judges. Prisoners condemned by the ICTY have been sent to such countries as Norway and Germany to do their time.

The ICTY statute does not allow for capital punishment. There is no record of any debate about this in the United Nations Security Council when the Tribunal was established, although at the time three of the permanent members, China, Russia, and the United States, all made regular use of the death penalty (Russia has now imposed a moratorium on capital punishment). When the statute was being adopted in 1993, some U.S. government officials felt that the imposition of the death penalty on those found guilty of crimes against humanity and genocide would promote the future rehabilitation of the former Yugoslavia. They argued that there was no question of the unfairness of such a penalty since capital punishment was provided for in the criminal code of Yugoslavia before the Balkan conflict began in 1991. Moreover, at the time, a majority of states still provided in their national criminal laws for the possibility of the death penalty for particularly serious crimes. Even those that have abolished the death penalty in recent years often maintain an exception for wartime offences. The Nuremberg Tribunal provided a precedent for imposing capital punishment for crimes under international law such as those covered by the ICTY statute. In fact, most of the defendants convicted by the Nuremberg Tribunal were sentenced to death, while the others received prison terms ranging from ten years to life. Finally, since the ICTY was expected to try the leading figures while lower-level perpetrators would be tried in domestic courts, there was a question of fairness, since the most culpable individuals would escape capital punishment whereas those who simply carried out their plans would be subject to the harshest of sentences.

But several important arguments supported the exclusion of capital punishment from the ICTY statute. The European members of the Security Council were strongly opposed to the death penalty. Indeed, a few months after the ICTY's establishment, the Council of Europe's Parliamentary Assembly adopted a resolution stating: "The Assembly considers that the death penalty has no legitimate place in the penal systems of modern civilized societies, and that its application may well be compared with torture." Moreover, the United Nations as an organization, particularly its human rights bodies, has been campaigning for the abolition of capital punishment for many years. The result has been steady progress in this direction. Shortly after the ICTY was established, the balance shifted internationally, and henceforth a majority of countries in the world have abolished capital punishment.

Furthermore, many countries now refuse to cooperate on matters of extradition and other forms of legal assistance if there is the prospect of capital punishment. For example, all European states and many in other parts of the world, including Canada, Mexico, and South Africa, will not send prisoners to the United States without an assurance that capital punishment will not be imposed. It would have been impossible for the Tribunal to operate properly if it allowed for the possibility of the death penalty. Even the United States, when the permanent International Criminal Court was being set up in 1998, opposed publicly the inclusion of capital punishment for precisely this reason.

Milosevic has been charged with all four categories of crimes that fall within the jurisdiction of the Yugoslavia Tribunal. The statute of the Tribunal does not give any specific indication of particular penalties for each type of crime. They are all subject, in principle, to the maximum of life imprisonment. But are some of them more serious than others? Some judges initially took the view that crimes against humanity were more serious than war crimes, although the majority now seems to consider that it is impossible to establish a hierarchy. Still, genocide would seem to be the supreme crime. It has led to the stiffest sentences to date, not only before the ICTY, in its single conviction for that crime (of forty-six years), but also before the International Criminal Tribunal for Rwanda.

Actually, the ICTY has yet to impose a sentence of life imprisonment, in contrast to its sister tribunal for Rwanda, where life sentences have been the rule. Instead, it has opted for increasingly lengthy prison terms. Perhaps the only logic in its approach is that, as it determines what appear to be increasingly serious levels of responsibility for ever more serious atrocities, it ups the ante a bit. The Tribunal's first major sentence, in the *Tadic* case, was twenty years. Then, in early 2000, dealing with the Croatian general Blaskic, it went to forty-five years. The following year, it sentenced a Serb general who had been implicated in the Srebrenica massacre, Radislav Krstic, to forty-six years. Slobodan Milosevic, if he is convicted, will likely be sentenced to forty-seven years, or more.

But what does it mean to sentence a sixty-year-old man to a term of this length? The statute seems to suggest that a prisoner can be paroled in accordance with the laws of the state of detention, "subject to the supervision of the International Tribunal." Yet the Tribunal is likely to go out of existence sometime in the next ten years or so. It is therefore unlikely to be able to play such a role in supervising sentences, except in the early years when parole should not be available in any case. No European state is going to allow lengthy imprisonment without the possibility of parole. A good indicator of best practice is the statute of the International Criminal Court, in which many countries, mainly in Europe and South America, insisted that life sentences could be allowed only if there was the possibility of parole after a maximum of twenty-five years' detention.

The probable outcome, then, is that, if convicted, Milosevic will be sentenced to a prison term in excess of forty-six years. This will be served in a Western European prison. But he will be considered eligible for parole after serving twenty-five years of the term. His pre-conviction detention is likely to be taken into account, so the term will be counted from late June 2001, when he was brought to The Hague, just a few weeks before his sixtieth birthday. Perhaps, then, Milosevic will be able to celebrate his eighty-fifth birthday enjoying a meal in a Belgrade café or giving interviews on late-night American television.

Prior to the war, even Yugoslavia did not allow for life imprisonment (although it occasionally imposed the death penalty), which it considered to be a form of cruel, inhuman, and degrading treatment or punishment. The maximum allowable sentence was twenty years in prison. For Americans, where harsh prison sentences, not to mention the death penalty, are common for serious crimes and where life sentences without the possibility of parole are regularly imposed, such sentencing may seem incredibly lenient. For Europeans, however, this approach seems to strike an appropriate balance between the need to make the punishment fit the crime and the imperative of humane treatment of detained persons.

Interminable Appeals

The actual trial of Milosevic is likely to last well into 2003, if not after. Then, depending upon the outcome, one or both sides can lodge an appeal. At that point, five judges of the Appeals Chamber, now presided over by a French judge and including judges from both the United States and Italy, will take over the case. If Milosevic thinks he has a grievance with the makeup of the Trial Chamber that hears his case first, he will be very unhappy with that of the Appeals Chamber.

Virtually every case to come before the ICTY to date has been appealed. For most of these cases, because there has been a conviction, but not on every charge the prosecutor listed in the indictment, both sides have appealed. The appeals have tended to reveal the mismatch between defense and prosecutor. The defendants complain that they have been denied a fair trial or else argue that the trial judges failed to properly assess the facts. The appeals judges have largely been unimpressed with such claims. The prosecutor, by contrast, has developed sophisticated arguments on points of law, and her success rate before the Appeals Chamber has been impressive.

But it is not unheard of for the Appeals Chamber to overturn a conviction where it finds that the facts have been grossly misinterpreted or when it judges the proceedings unfair. It did this in October 2001, in the *Kupreskic* case, after allowing new evidence on appeal. The Appeals Chamber considered that the original indictment had been vague and overly general, with the result that the defendants were at an unfair disadvantage.

From beginning to end, the trial and appeal process can take two, three, even four years. But that is not the end of it. Even when definitively sentenced by the Appeals Chamber, defendants continue to fight using a range of postconviction remedies. This may involve an attempt to produce new evidence or a claim that misbehavior by the prosecutor or even by defense counsel jeopardized the right to a fair trial. The very first case to be tried by the Tribunal, that of Dusko Tadic, is still not finished. Tadic appealed his conviction, but the final judgment was not issued until some four years after the proceedings had begun. Then, when it was established that one of his lawyers acted improperly, he asked for the case to be heard again. That application is now pending.

Implications for Future Wars

That Milosevic could be brought to trial for war crimes and similar outrages committed while he was president of a sovereign state is not in itself anything groundbreaking in international law. As early as 1919 the victorious allies planned to try the German emperor, Kaiser Wilhelm, though they were never able to get their hands on him and actually hold the trial. Both Nuremberg and Tokyo reaffirmed the principle. And there is more recently, the Pinochet precedent. In 1999 English courts refused to entertain the former Chilean dictator's argument that as a former head of state he was immune from prosecution because any alleged crimes had been committed while he was in office.

Perhaps what is new about the Milosevic case is that he was actually indicted by the court while in office. In other words, the charges and the threat of prosecution and conviction may actually have influenced the outcome of the war. That, at any rate, is the theory. There are good arguments on both sides of this deterrence debate. Those who believe in the deterrent effect of criminal prosecution hold to the view that the Milosevic prosecution will discourage offenders in the future. Those who discount deterrence recall Louise Arbour standing on the border of Kosovo in January 1999 and threatening Milosevic with prosecution if he didn't behave. It had no discernable effect on the ethnic cleansing that followed or on the war itself.

But in a more general sense, there can be little doubt that, with the increasing acceptance of international prosecution for war crimes, crimes against humanity, and genocide, we have entered a new age in the promotion of international peace and security. In the past, even if there was a theoretical possibility of prosecution, the chances of it actually coming to pass were about as good as being struck by lightning. Now, while not a certainty, it is more and more likely that those leaders who commit war crimes or persecute civilian populations will be called to account. Prosecution may not have deterred Milosevic, but the example his prosecution sets will help to deter others in the future.

The International Criminal Court

The creation of the Yugoslavia Tribunal was in many ways a byproduct of ongoing work within the United Nations aimed at creating a permanent international criminal court. The idea had been revived in 1989 after lying dormant during the Cold War. While the activity was still in its early stages, the Yugoslav war broke out. The idea of a court was too good to resist, but nobody could wait for the permanent court to be established. In July 1998, at a diplomatic conference convened in Rome, 120 states voted in favor of a treaty that is to create the International Criminal Court. The Rome statute, as it is called, requires sixty state ratifications before it actually comes into effect. By February 2002, when the Milosevic trial began, the statute had obtained fifty-two. On April 11, 2002, the sixtieth ratification was deposited, bringing the Rome statute into force.

In the mid-1990s, while the ICTY was struggling to catch defendants and determine its procedure and practice, work on the proposed international court plodded along. Indeed, the experience of the International Criminal Tribunal actually contributed to this parallel process. Some of the provisions that were later adopted in the Rome statute reflected lessons learned in The Hague. Sometimes the negotiators tried to readjust the law a bit, reflecting their dissatisfaction with some aspects of the approach taken by the ICTY's often bold and imaginative rulings. For example, in its first important judgment, the Appeals Chamber gave an extremely broad reading of the ICTY Statute's provisions dealing with the types of crimes covered. While this seemed to ensure that defendants would not slip through some loopholes, it terrified officials in many countries who feared that judges of the future international court, where they might themselves appear as defendants, could run amok. The result was a provision requiring that crimes be "strictly construed."

The new International Criminal Court is designed to apply throughout the world, unlike the *ad hoc* tribunals that cover only the territories of the former Yugoslavia and Rwanda. But because the International Criminal Court is being created by treaty, not by resolution of the UN Security Council, it can only apply to those countries that agree. The International Criminal Court will be able to prosecute cases that arise within countries that have ratified the Rome statute, as well as cases involving their citizens, wherever the crime is committed. Already that will cover a good part of the world and should ensure that the court has plenty of work. Critics of this approach claimed that the court would never be able to operate effectively, because only countries where civil conflict was unknown or improbable would ever ratify the Rome statute. One of the more stunning developments in the ratification process, however, has been the willingness of countries actually engaged in conflict, or emerging from a period of civil strife, to join the court.

The first examples were Fiji and Sierra Leone. Both had been through periods of civil war or unrest literally within months of ratifying the Rome statute. They were followed by several of the Balkan states, including the Federal Republic of Yugoslavia, and by a troubled African state, Nigeria. As ratification progressed, it became clear that countries like Burundi, the Democratic Republic of Congo, and Colombia, all of them afflicted with what seems like endemic armed conflict, were seriously considering joining the court.

The significance of this development cannot be underestimated and may, ultimately, be the lasting legacy of the Milosevic prosecution. These countries seem convinced that the threat of prosecution for war crimes, crimes against humanity, and even genocide, even imposed on their own generals and political leaders, can help to bring peace. At any rate, frustrated by interminable conflict and the apparent inability of international organizations like the United Nations, the African Union, the Organization for Security and Cooperation in Europe, and the Organization of American States to help in resolving matters, they seem prepared to give the International Criminal Court a chance. If they had genuinely believed the Yugoslavia Tribunal to be ineffective, they would hardly have taken such a course.

Aggression: The Crime That Defies Definition

In his courtroom outbursts, Milosevic has charged NATO states with aggression against Yugoslavia. The failure of the ICTY to proceed against NATO leaders for waging war against Yugoslavia strikes many as a case of unfairness and of selective prosecution. But the ICTY is powerless to deal with cases of illegal war. It can prosecute only crimes committed during a war, not the crime of waging illegal war.

The situation was different at Nuremberg. There, the Nazi leaders were charged not only with war crimes and crimes against humanity but also with "crimes against peace." Indeed, when they convicted the defendants, the Nuremberg judges described the waging of illegal war as "the supreme international crime, differing only from other war crimes in that it contains within itself the accumulated evil of the whole." But lingering uncertainty about where "crimes against peace" actually fit within the general scheme of crimes arose at sentencing. The Nuremberg judges could not bring themselves to impose the ultimate penalty, execution by hanging, upon defendants who were convicted only of crimes against peace, like Rudolf Hess, and not of war crimes and crimes against humanity. However, the one defendant who was convicted of crimes against humanity alone, Julius Streicher, was sentenced to death and actually executed.

One of the significant differences between the statute of the Yugoslavia Tribunal and that of the International Criminal Court is the possibility of prosecuting the crime of "aggression," which is a more modern formulation of what the Nuremberg court called "crimes against peace." Why did the Security Council not include the crime of aggression within the subject matter jurisdiction of the Yugoslavia Tribunal? Its principle concern, reflected in the work of the Commission of Experts that preceded the Tribunal's creation, was with the atrocities being committed on all sides, rather than with determining who started the war. And at the time, the commission probably never imagined what became a reality at the end of the decade, namely, a confrontation between the Federal Republic of Yugoslavia and NATO that would be subject to the court's jurisdiction.

But while the crime of aggression figures in the Rome statute, the new International Criminal Court will not immediately be able to prosecute under this count. The diplomatic conference was unable to agree upon a definition of *aggression* or on the technical aspects of how it would be prosecuted. In a last-minute compromise designed to appease states which insisted that aggression be covered, the delegations decided to recognize the crime as part of the court's jurisdiction, but subject to future agreement. Cynics say the reference to aggression in the statute of the International Criminal Court is no more than a placeholder.

Talks are now underway, and the subject is far from easy. There is a vast range of possible definitions: on one extreme, anything falling short of full-blown invasion and occupation by a foreign army is not deemed to be aggression; on the other extreme, it can consist of mere border incidents. Here, consensus will not be easy to achieve. But there is an additional issue. According to the Charter of the United Nations, it is the Security Council that has primary responsibility for determining cases of aggression. The permanent members of the Security Council are loath to accept any encroachment upon their prerogatives in this respect. Certainly any suggestion that NATO forces had committed aggression against the Federal Republic of Yugoslavia during the 1999 bombing campaign would not make it past the veto in the Security Council, which has three NATO states among its permanent members, namely the United States, the United Kingdom, and France.

For some, the failure of international justice to address the question of aggression shows its fundamental hypocrisy. They argue that what the Nuremberg judges called the "supreme crime" has fallen off the radar screen in order to appease the great military powers that sit as permanent members of the Security Council. For others, prosecuting aggression is a distraction from the main task of international justice, which is to address atrocities committed against civilian populations. Holding civilian and military leaders accountable for the crimes they perpetrate against their own people, particularly ethnic minorities and other vulnerable groups, is the *raison d'etre* of the exercise.

Accountability, Truth, and Reconciliation

Yugoslavia, Croatia, and Bosnia and Herzegovina are all engaged in the process of rebuilding after years of brutal war. Atrocities were committed on all sides in this intensely cosmopolitan country. Somehow, they will have to find a way to live with one another, whether it be within genuinely multiethnic states or simply as good neighbors. Even where ethnic cleansing was most effective, there remain minorities, and, with the legal right of relocated people to return, some of the worst of the cleansing may be partially reversed. Will the Milosevic trial, and more generally, the work of the Yugoslavia Tribunal, contribute to this process?

One of the premises that underlies the Yugoslavia Tribunal is a belief that accountability for war crimes and other atrocities is essential to peace and reconciliation. Unhealed wounds dating to World War II and even before are cited as being among the causes of the conflicts. Only when crimes are addressed, it is said, and only when justice is seen to be done, can societies move forward. But this is a controversial proposition for those who urge victims to "forgive and forget."

All around the world, some process of accountability is being urged as a way of coping with civil strife and ethnic conflict. The mechanisms vary. In some cases, criminal prosecution has taken a back seat to innovative approaches like so-called "truth commissions." The most celebrated of these was the South African Truth and Reconciliation Commission, presided by Archbishop Desmond Tutu. Elsewhere, for example in Sierra Leone, truth commissions have been presented not as an alternative to criminal justice but rather as its complement.

Inspired by the South African model, a truth commission has been proposed for Bosnia and Herzegovina for several years. The idea was initially opposed by the prosecutor of the Yugoslavia Tribunal, who felt it would interfere with her ongoing prosecutions. Opinions have mellowed since then, and it is now widely accepted that a truth commission will contribute to the peace and reconciliation process, both in Bosnia and Herzegovina and in the Federal

Republic of Yugoslavia itself. But in Kosovo, where ethnic hatred is still very much common currency, the prospect of such alternative approaches is still remote.

Several countries are now experimenting with what are called "internationalized tribunals." These are hybrids, grafted onto national justice systems but with a very important international input in terms of personnel, money, and law. Examples here include the Serious Crimes Chamber of the United Nations administration in East Timor and the Special Court for Sierra Leone. The International Criminal Tribunal for the former Yugoslavia fits within this range of initiatives. Viewed from this perspective, we understand that its objectives go beyond simply identification of individual offenders and their prosecution and punishment. Of course, it is convincingly argued that one of the benefits of the criminal justice route in such a context is that it does in fact individualize responsibility. It is not a people as a whole that is stigmatized but rather an individual leader or some powerful clique.

And yet the trial of Slobodan Milosevic is about far more than assessing the alleged antisocial behavior of a single criminal. It is also about determining historical truth. This is where the trial's mission seems to overlap with other mechanisms, like truth commissions. We can see this at Nuremberg. The names of most of those who were convicted, not to mention their specific contribution to the Nazi regime, have been long forgotten. But the judgment of the International Military Tribunal stands as a landmark, documenting the atrocities of the SS, the Gestapo, and the other components of Nazi leadership. Hitler was not a defendant—in fact, he was dead before the trial began—and yet he stands convicted, albeit indirectly, by the Nuremberg judgment.

The Milosevic trial promises to be much the same. The defendant himself—defiant and provocative—stands as the supreme example of an extreme nationalist regime that took power in the former Yugoslavia and that presided over its breakup. In an attempt to resist the collapse of the state and then, when this seemed certain, to reconfigure the boundaries along real or imagined ethnic lines, horrible atrocities were committed against civilian populations. Whether this was simply the work of isolated rogues, something we see in almost all armed conflict, or was ordered from the top is what the trial will determine.

The question we cannot answer here is whether the process and the verdict can contribute to peace in Yugoslavia. Clearly, we must be prepared for a range of outcomes, including acquittal. Will an assessment of the brutal history of Yugoslavia by three judges from outside the Balkans, skilled jurists all of them but acknowledged amateurs when it comes to history and politics, help the fractured country to recover? We recall the words of former Chinese premier Chou En-Lai who, when asked whether the French Revolution had been a success, famously replied: "It's too early to tell."

GLOSSARY OF KEY LEGAL TERMS

Abetted, see Aided and abetted.

Actus reus. The material or objective element of a crime, from the Latin for "guilty act." The prosecutor must establish that the accused was responsible for the material act, or *actus reus,* that is involved in the crime but also that the offender had knowledge of the relevant facts and intent to commit the act (known as *mens rea*).

Additional Protocols to the Geneva Conventions of 1977. Two treaties adopted to bring the 1949 Geneva Conventions up to date, particularly in light of post–World War II conflicts like the Vietnam war. Protocol I deals with international armed conflict, and Protocol II deals with noninternational armed conflict. Serious violations of the two protocols can be prosecuted as "violations of the laws or customs of war" under Article 3 of the ICTY Statute.

Admissibility. A preliminary issue for the tribunal, consisting of a verification that it has the authority to try the case and that there is no other impediment to a trial, such as a claim of double jeopardy. Admissibility also refers to whether or not the trial chamber will allow evidence to be presented in court.

Adversarial system, see Common law.

Affidavit. A written statement taken while the affiant, deponent, or witness has sworn an oath to tell the truth. Strict common law rules of evidence do not, as a general rule, allow affidavit evidence in a criminal trial. But at Nuremberg, affidavits were widely admitted as a replacement for live testimony, a subject of much criticism. Where the content is not particularly controversial and where the evidence appears reliable, they can be admitted before the ICTY.

Aggravating factors. Factors to be taken into account in sentencing that tend to lengthen a sentence. Examples include a superior or commanding position in a hierarchy and evidence of premeditation where this is not a specific element of the crime itself. The opposite of mitigating factors.

Aided and abetted. Expression used in article 7 of the ICTY statute to describe what is sometimes called "complicity." An individual is responsible for a crime even if he or she does not actually commit the physical criminal act. The accomplice must either aid, by performing a material act that assists the principal perpetrator, or abet, by encouraging the perpetrator.

***Amicus curiae*.** Literally, a "friend of the court." The *amicus curiae* (plural, *amici curiae*) may be appointed by the court or may volunteer. *Amici* advise the court, usually on legal issues. To ensure that legal issues are not presented in a one-sided manner, given that Milosevic has refused to be represented by counsel before the ICTY, the trial chamber has invited the registrar (see Registry) to designate one or more *amici curiae*. Three distinguished international criminal lawyers, Steven Kay QC, G. Branislav Tapuskovic, and Professor Mischa Wladimiroff were subsequently appointed.

Appeals Chamber. A five-judge panel with the authority to overturn decisions of the trial chamber and to order an acquittal or a retrial, or to revise a sentencing judgment. It is the court of last resort because there is no "supreme court." The appeals chamber has already ruled on preliminary aspects of the Milosevic case, for example, in its January 31, 2002 judgment overturning the trial chamber's decision that separate trials be held for the various indictments against Milosevic.

Armed conflict. The resort to armed force between states, or protracted armed violence between governmental authorities and organized armed groups or between such groups within a state.

International humanitarian law distinguishes between international and noninternational, or internal, armed conflict.

Attempt. Only in the case of genocide can the ICTY prosecute the attempt to commit an offense where it does not actually take place. But to date, it has charged no one, including Milosevic, with attempted genocide. The ICTY has had its hands full going after crimes that were fully consummated without having to devote energy to "attempts."

Binding Order, see Order.

Bureau. A body within the ICTY composed of the president, the vice-president, and the presiding judges of the trial chambers. The bureau can take decisions on the disqualification of judges and on a variety of essentially administrative matters.

Chambers. A collective reference to the judges of the tribunal. The ICTY is divided into several trial chambers and one appeals chamber.

Charter of the United Nations. The constitution of the United Nations organization, proclaimed on the stage of the San Francisco Opera in June 1945. Because the security council decided to create the international criminal tribunal for the former Yugoslavia, under article 25 of the charter, all member states are required to comply with it. The security council considered the Tribunal to be an appropriate measure to deal with international peace and security, using its enforcement powers set out in Chapter VII of the charter. The legitimacy of its view has been confirmed in several decisions of the ICTY.

Civil law system, see Romano-Germanic system.

Civil law. A commonly used expression to describe the procedural regime used in criminal trials in continental Europe and many other parts of the world, characterized by an inquisitorial approach rather than the adversarial framework of the common law.

Civil war, see noninternational armed conflict.

Civilian population. Crimes against humanity must consist of an attack on a "civilian population." The adjective *civilian* is defined broadly and is meant to emphasize the collective nature of the crimes amounting to crimes against humanity rather than strictly the status of the victims. It covers not only civilians in a strict sense but also all persons who were no longer combatants, whether due to injury or because they were off duty while the crimes were committed.

Closing argument. A trial takes place in two phases, the first involving the production of evidence, the second in which the two sides attempt to draw conclusions about issues of law and fact and explain the theory of their case to the judges. The prosecutor goes first, but even if he or she has nothing to say, the defense may then make a closing argument. The prosecutor can present a rebuttal argument, to which the defense may present a rejoinder.

Command responsibility. A legal technique by which a commander or superior may be convicted of crimes committed by his or her subordinates, even if the prosecution cannot prove that the commander or superior actually knew of the crimes or in some way ordered or incited them. In effect, the commander or superior is punished for providing negligent supervision of subordinates. The concept was first developed in post–World War II trials and was later codified in Additional Protocol I to the Geneva Conventions of 1977.

Common design. A form of complicity where offenders have a common design; that is, they possess the same criminal intention to commit a specific act and formulate a plan to carry it out, although each coperpetrator may play a different role within it.

Common law. The procedural system that first developed in England and then spread to its colonies, almost all of which kept the system with some modifications after decolonization. The common law treats prosecutor and defense as adversaries who in effect duel before relatively passive judges. Each side takes strategic decisions aimed at winning its case rather than approaching the trial as a forum where the truth of the allegations is to be determined in an objective sense.

Commutation. A penalty imposed by the tribunal may later be subject to commutation, that is, reduction or even cancellation, in accordance with the laws that apply to the state where sentence is being served.

Compensation. The tribunal itself cannot order compensation to victims, but its judgments are sent to states so as to facilitate claims for compensation by victims under national legislation. In some countries, a criminal conviction also establishes the liability of the offender in terms of compensation to victims. The tribunal's judgment should be treated as such a decision under national law.

Competence. This term is sometimes used as a synonym for jurisdiction. It refers to the power or authority of the tribunal to judge cases, rather than to its ability.

Complicity. Participation in a crime for which the main physical act is committed by another. Accomplices general participate by "aiding and abetting" the commission of specific acts. But an accomplice may also be held liable for acts of other participants that are reasonably foreseeable when there is an overall plan or common design to carry out a criminal act. Milosevic is charged as an accomplice to a variety of acts. He is also specifically charged with complicity in the crime of genocide as part of the Kosovo indictment.

Concurrent jurisdiction. War crimes, genocide, and crimes against humanity can be prosecuted before a number of courts besides the ICTY. These include the national courts of the states of the former Yugoslavia, but also many courts in Europe and elsewhere that allow prosecution on the basis of universal jurisdiction. This is concurrent jurisdiction. But in case of conflict, the ICTY takes precedence under the principle of "Primacy."

Concurrent sentences. If two or more convictions are registered by the trial chamber it may impose distinct sentences for each crime yet order that they be served concurrently, especially if they relate to the same general fact situation or criminal transaction. In practice, then, the convicted person serves the longer of the two sentences. Alternatively, the trial chamber may specify that the sentences be served consecutively. There is no limit in the statute as to the length of sentences. The longest imposed to date is forty-six years.

Conspiracy. An agreement between two or more persons to commit a crime. Under the tribunal's statute, the principle of conspiracy is applicable only to the charge of genocide.

Contempt. Misconduct before the tribunal may be punished by it as "contempt." Contempt includes such acts as "contumaciously" refusing or failing to answer a question, violating orders of the tribunal, and tampering with witnesses.

Counsel. An accused and even a suspect may designate a lawyer or advocate. Such counsel must file proof that they have been appointed, in the form of a power of attorney or mandate. Counsel should satisfy the registrar (see Registry) that he or she is admitted to the practice of law in a state, or is a university professor of law, and speaks one of the two working languages of the tribunal, English or French.

Crimes against humanity. The concept of crimes against humanity was first recognized at the Nuremberg trial. It filled a major gap in humanitarian law, which hitherto had regarded what a state did to its own population as being its own concern, in contrast with what a state did to populations of occupied territories or soldiers of another belligerent, who were already protected by existing rules. Crimes against humanity consist of an underlying "ordinary crime," like murder, that is committed as part of a widespread or systematic attack on a civilian population. Despite the terms of the ICTY Statute, which allows prosecution only for crimes against humanity committed during international or internal armed conflict, the Tribunal has said that customary international law imposes no such requirement, and that crimes against humanity can be committed even in peacetime. This conclusion was confirmed in the Rome statute for the international criminal court (see Rome statute).

Cruel treatment. A grave breach of the 1949 Geneva Conventions and a violation of common Article 3 of the Conventions, involving infliction of severe physical or mental pain or suffering upon one or more persons.

Cumulative convictions. Although the prosecutor is free to charge an accused with several different offenses concerning the same act, if there is a conviction, the tribunal will enter a finding of guilt only with respect to one offense if there is sufficient overlap. For example, Milosevic is charged with the violations of the laws and customs of war of both "torture" and "cruel treatment" during the conflict in

Bosnia and Herzegovina. If the tribunal concludes he is responsible for both crimes, it will enter only a conviction for torture.

Customary international law. A source of international law derived not from written treaties but rather from unwritten rules developed over the ages. Customary law is established by proof of constant practice by states indicating the existence of a legal rule, coupled with some indication (other than the practice itself) that they consider themselves to be bound by such a rule. Judges at the ICTY consider that the crimes defined in the statute should be interpreted in light of the state of customary law at the time the tribunal was established or the crime committed, and not go beyond it. But they have also noted that in some respects the statute falls short of customary law, for example, in its unnecessary requirement that crimes against humanity be committed as part of an armed conflict.

Customs of war. Half of the expression "laws or customs of war." International law is an amalgam of customary law (see Customary international law) and treaties. These two sources are reflected in the concept "laws or customs of war."

Decision, see Order.

Defense. The accused or the accused's counsel.

Deportation. A crime against humanity involving the forced displacement of a civilian population by expulsion or other coercive acts from the area in which it is lawfully present.

Deposition. Testimony by a witness taken out of court, sometimes by videoconference, but for use during the trial as if the witness were actually present. The trial chamber can authorize a deposition in cases where a witness cannot physically attend or for other reasons deemed acceptable.

Disclosure. Prior to trial, the prosecutor is required to disclose or make available to the defense copies of witness statements of those who will be called to testify, copies of sworn statements, books, documents, photographs, and tangible objects that are material to the defense. The prosecutor can ask the trial chamber to make exceptions to this general obligation.

Disqualification. Removal of a judge assigned to a case because the judge has a personal interest or has or has had any association that might affect his or her impartiality.

Double jeopardy, see *Non bis in idem.*

Due process. Ancient term of the common law referring to the right to a fair trial.

Duress. A defense invoked by the accused during trial whereby the commission of the criminal act is admitted, but it is claimed that the perpetrator had no moral choice because he or she was threatened with death or some other dire consequence. In a very divided judgment, the Appeals Chamber ruled that duress was no defense to a charge of crimes against humanity. But the Rome statute, adopted a year after that judgment, allows the defense, indicating that most countries prefer the view of the dissenting judges whereby duress is permitted in certain circumstances.

Duty judge. A single judge, designated by the president, who can take certain urgent decisions.

Enslavement. A crime against humanity involving the exercise of any or all of the powers attaching to the right of ownership over a person, such as by purchasing, selling, lending, or bartering such a person or persons, including the exercise of such power in the course of trafficking in persons, in particular women and children.

Equality of arms. Concept developed in human rights law whereby a fair trial requires that both sides, Prosecution and Defense, have a certain equivalence in terms of resources.

Ethnic group. One of the groups protected by the prohibition of Genocide. It is similar in many respects to a national or racial group. In its consideration of the crime of Genocide, the ICTY has treated the Bosnian Muslims as an ethnic group rather than as a national or racial group.

Ex parte. Latin term used to describe a proceeding at which one or even both of the parties is not present. For example, if one of the parties asks the Tribunal to order a state to produce evidence, the state in question may argue that this will compromise its national security interests. It can do so during an *ex parte* hearing at which neither Prosecutor nor Defense can attend.

Expert witness. A witness who ventures an opinion about a matter that is beyond the expertise of the judges themselves.

Extermination. A crime against humanity by which a particular Civilian population is targeted for death, either by killing or being otherwise subjected to conditions of life calculated to bring about the destruction of a numerically significant part of the population. Milosevic is charged with extermination in the indictments concerning Croatia and Bosnia and Herzegovina, but not with respect to Kosovo.

Extradition. Process by which an accused is sent from one state to another in order to stand trial. The ICTY prefers to speak of "transfer" to describe rendition of an accused to The Hague.

General Assembly. One of the principal organs of the United Nations, this body is more representative than the Security Council but has little real power. Milosevic and others have argued that it is the General Assembly, not the Security Council, that has the power to establish an international criminal tribunal. But this argument was dismissed long ago in a definitive ruling of the appeals chamber. In any case, the General Assembly has willingly participated in the tribunal's activities, approving its budget and electing its judges.

Geneva Conventions. Four international treaties adopted in 1949 to deal with the protection of victims of armed conflict: wounded soldiers and sailors, prisoners of war, and civilians. In principle applicable only to international armed conflict, each of the four conventions includes one provision, known as "common Article 3," addressing the protection of victims of noninternational armed conflict.

Genocide. The intentional destruction of a national, ethnic, racial, or religious group, in whole or in part. The definition of genocide in article 4 of the ICTY Statute is taken essentially word for word from the 1948 Convention on the Prevention and Punishment of the Crime of Genocide. It has been described by judges as the "crime of crimes" and is, arguably, the most severe of the four categories of crimes within the tribunal's jurisdiction. Genocide is in many ways an extreme form of the crime against humanity of persecution, to which it is closely related.

Grave breaches. Grave breaches consist of particularly heinous violations of the 1949 Geneva Conventions and of Additional Protocol I. They are punishable under article 2 of the ICTY Statute. Grave breaches can only be committed in international armed conflict. All states have an obligation to investigate grave breaches and see that their perpetrators are brought to justice, wherever the crimes have been committed.

Habeas corpus. A remedy by which a person who is detained challenges the legality of the detention. Though not explicitly provided for in the ICTY Rules of procedure and evidence, judges of the tribunal will consider a motion of *habeas corpus.*

Hague Convention. International treaty adopted in 1907 that concerns the laws or customs of war. It largely codifies important customary legal rules dealing with means and methods of war, the protection of prisoners, and the rights of civilians in an occupied territory. Though not designed as a criminal law treaty, its prohibitions were taken as the basis of individual criminal responsibility by the Nuremberg Tribunal. Violations of the Hague Convention are included in article 3 of the ICTY Statute.

Head of state or government. Many countries grant their own heads of state or government a form of immunity from criminal prosecution, at the very least while they are still in office. However, no similar immunity was recognized at Nuremberg in the case of international prosecution. Milosevic is the first sitting head of state or government to be prosecuted by an international tribunal.

Human rights law. Body of international law developed since World War II in such instruments as the Universal Declaration of Human Rights, the Convention on the Prevention and Punishment of the Crime of Genocide, and the international human rights covenants. The ICTY has often referred to precedents from human rights bodies like the European Court of Human Rights, particularly with respect to fair trial issues.

Humanitarian law. Sometimes called "international humanitarian law," or "IHL," this is the body of law that regulates armed conflict, both international and noninternational. The core of humanitarian law consists of the four Geneva Conventions of 1949, the two Additional Protocols of 1977, and the Hague Convention of 1907. The Statute of the ICTY says it is to prosecute "serious violations of international humanitarian law."

ICTY. The International Criminal Tribunal for the Former Yugoslavia.

Imprisonment. A crime against humanity consisting of severe deprivation of liberty, usually involving inhumane conditions. Milosevic is charged with this offense in respect of prison camps located in Montenegro, Serbia, and Bosnia and Herzegovina.

***In camera* proceedings.** Proceedings that are not public.

Incitement. Incitement to commit genocide can be prosecuted by the ICTY even if no one is actually incited to commit the crime. But Milosevic is not charged with incitement to commit genocide. He is charged under the closely related concepts of instigating and abetting, both of which require evidence that the underlying crime was actually committed by others.

Indictment. The indictment is prepared by the prosecutor and sets out the charges against the accused. It must be in sufficient detail to indicate the points that are at issue and not to take the accused by surprise at trial. Milosevic is charged under three distinct indictments, one concerning the civil war in Kosovo in early 1999, a second dealing with the war that followed Croatia's secession from the Socialist Federal Republic of Yugoslavia in mid-1991, and a third dealing with the war in Bosnia and Herzegovina that took place from April 1992 until the Dayton Peace Agreement in late 1995.

Inhumane Acts. A crime against humanity involving infliction of great suffering or serious injury to body or to mental or physical health, by means of any act similar in nature to those set out in the list of crimes against humanity, such as Murder, sexual violence, torture, and beatings. Milosevic is charged with inhumane acts in all three indictments.

Inquisitorial system, see Romano-Germanic system.

Intent. It is a requirement for any criminal conviction that the prohibited act be committed with intent and knowledge, often referred to by the Latin expression *Mens rea* or guilty mind.

Interlocutory motion. An issue contested during the proceedings, usually on procedural or evidentiary issues, and on which one of the parties seeks an immediate ruling. Normally judgments on interlocutory motions are not subject to appeal.

Internal armed conflict, see Noninternational armed conflict.

International armed conflict. Resort to armed force by two or more states. Certain violations of international humanitarian law that are within the jurisdiction of the ICTY, notably grave breaches of the Geneva Conventions, can be prosecuted only if it can be shown that there was an international armed conflict. The prosecutor is alleging that with the secession of Croatia as well as Bosnia and Herzegovina from the Socialist Federal Republic of Yugoslavia, the armed conflicts that followed were international in nature. Although the Kosovo war of March–June 1999 was undoubtedly international in nature, given the NATO bombing raids, Milosevic is charged only with respect to the noninternational armed conflict that raged between Kosovo Albanian forces and the armed forces and militias directed by the Belgrade government.

International Court of Justice. Neighbor of the ICTY in The Hague, the International Court of Justice hears cases between sovereign states, in contrast to the ICTY, which is concerned with cases directed against individuals. Three cases concerning the wars in Yugoslavia are currently pending before the International Court of Justice, one by Bosnia and Herzegovina against the Federal Republic of Yugoslavia (and vice versa) alleging genocide, a second by the Federal Republic of Yugoslavia against several NATO powers charging both genocide and illegal use of force during the Kosovo bombing campaign, and a third by Croatia against the Federal Republic of Yugoslavia alleging genocide during the 1991 war.

International Criminal Court, see Rome statute.

Joinder. Persons accused of the same or different crimes committed in the course of the same transaction may be jointly charged and tried. Milosevic is jointly charged with four others in the Kosovo Indictment, but because his coaccused have not been apprehended he is being tried alone. Also, two or more crimes may be joined in one indictment if the series of acts committed together form the same transaction and the crimes were committed by the same accused.

Milosevic is charged with a range of specific crimes in each of the three Indictments.

Joint criminal enterprise. A venture by two or more persons to effect a criminal result, in which each member is held responsible for the specific acts perpetrated by the other members of the enterprise, but only to the extent the venture was likely to lead to such an act. Where a defendant is charged with a crime committed by another participant that goes beyond the agreed object of the joint criminal enterprise, the prosecutor must establish that the crime was a natural and foreseeable consequence of the enterprise and that the accused was aware of this when he or she agreed to participate in the enterprise

Joint trial. A trial of two or more accused.

Judgment. Ruling by the judges of the trial chamber or by a majority of them at the conclusion of the trial on the question of guilt or innocence. The judgment may also determine that property was taken unlawfully. The final determination of an appeal by the appeals chamber is also called a judgment.

Judicial notice. As a general rule, if the judges are to take facts into account in their deliberations such facts must be proven in open court. But some facts are so notorious and well accepted that judges may take "judicial notice" of them. The ICTY judges have refused to take judicial notice of the fact that an international or noninternational armed conflict took place in the former Yugoslavia.

Jurisdiction. The limits that circumscribe the power of the tribunal. See also: subject matter jurisdiction, personal jurisdiction, temporal jurisdiction, and territorial jurisdiction.

Killing, see Murder.

Laws of war. Historic rules governing means and methods of warfare and the treatment of wounded, prisoners, and civilians. Many of them date back to the age of chivalry, and they are regularly referred to in classical Greek histories as well as in the plays of Shakespeare. The first great modern codification is the Hague Convention of 1907. They were referred to as part of the expression "laws or customs of war" in article 6(b) of the charter of the Nuremberg Tribunal.

Pursuant to article 3 of the Statute, the ICTY has jurisdiction over "laws or customs of war," and Milosevic faces several counts of this offense.

Lawyer-client privilege. Communications between lawyer and client are privileged and cannot be disclosed at trial without the consent of the client, unless the client has voluntarily disclosed the content of the communication to a third party and that third party then gives evidence of that disclosure.

Martens clause. So-named after its author, a Russian diplomat, who insisted that a clause be added to the preamble of the 1907 Hague Convention, recognizing that inhumane acts, even those not codified by the treaty, remain prohibited: "Until a more complete code of the laws of war has been issued, the High Contracting Parties deem it expedient to declare that, in cases not included in the regulations adopted by them, the inhabitants and the belligerents remain under the protection and the rule of the principles of the law of nations, as they result from the usages established among civilized peoples, from the laws of humanity, and the dictates of the public conscience."

Material element, see *Actus reus.*

Mens rea. The mental or subjective element of a crime, from the Latin for "guilty mind." A guilty act (or *Actus reus*) is punishable as a crime only if the offender had knowledge of the relevant facts or circumstances and actually intended to commit the act. But this should not be confused with motive, which is the reason why the act was committed. For most crimes, the tribunal does not require proof of motive, although it may find such evidence to be helpful in clarifying any doubts about whether the accused actually committed the crime. But in the case of the crime against humanity of persecution, with which Milosevic is charged in all three indictments, the prosecutor must establish that he did this on "political, racial and religious grounds" or, in other words, for a discriminatory motive.

Military necessity. A justification for the commission of war crimes in certain circumstances. For example, wanton destruction of cities, towns, or villages or devastation is a violation of the laws or customs of war, but only to the extent it is not justified by military necessity (see article 3[b]). Milosevic is charged with wanton destruction and plunder of homes and religious and cultural buildings belonging to non-Serb populations, but only to the extent this was not justified by "military necessity," throughout Bosnia and Herzegovina, including Banja Luka, Bihac, Foca, Sarajevo, Prijedor, Srebrenica, and Zvornik.

Mitigating factors. So that the punishment actually fits the crime, an accused may invoke a range of personal circumstances, including age, infirmity, and mental illness in order to reduce the sentence that might otherwise be imposed. The statute makes specific reference to superior orders as a factor in mitigation (but not a defense), but it equally excludes official position—the situation of Slobodan Milosevic—as a mitigating element. See also Aggravating factors.

Moot question. A legal or factual issue that is no longer of any consequence with respect to the result of the case.

Motion to acquit. At the conclusion of the prosecutor's evidence, the defense may ask the trial chamber for an immediate acquittal on the grounds that the prosecutor has not proven all of the essential elements of the charge. If the motion is dismissed, the defense must decide whether to call for evidence.

Motion. An application to the tribunal that normally takes place prior to or during the trial, asking the judges to make a ruling on a specific issue. Motions may deal with the admissibility of evidence or with a variety of procedural questions. A motion is not generally subject to appeal to the appeals chamber.

Motive. The reason why a crime is committed, as opposed to the intent, which is quite a distinct concept. Several people may all intend to commit a crime, but for different motives. Generally, motive is not an element to be considered in assessing guilt or innocence, although judges tend to be more easily convinced of guilt when they can understand why a person committed a crime and to be equally perplexed about guilt when they see no reason why a person committed a crime. The statute introduces a motive requirement with respect to the crime against humanity of persecution, which must be committed on "political, racial and religious grounds."

Murder. The statute refers to both "murder" and "killing." This is for historical reasons, because the crimes defined in the statute are derived from various texts that use slightly different terminology. But the tribunal has concluded that the grave breach and genocidal act of "killing" and the crime against humanity of "murder" amount to the same thing: intentional homicide.

National court. A court that is part of the justice system established by the legislation of a sovereign state. National courts have concurrent jurisdiction with the ICTY. An arrangement exists by which the national courts of Bosnia and Herzegovina prosecute only violations of humanitarian law after consultation with and authorization by the office of the prosecutor of the ICTY.

National group. A category of group protected by the prohibition of Genocide. The ICTY, in its only judgment on this issue, has considered Bosnian Muslims to be an "Ethnic group" rather than a "national group."

***Nicaragua* decision.** A 1985 ruling of the International Court of Justice dealing with involvement of *contras,* backed by the United States, in the civil war in Nicaragua. The court established a criterion of "effective control" in determining whether acts of armed bands acting within a country could be imputed to a foreign power. In a case dealing with the level of control that the Federal Republic of Yugoslavia exercised over Bosnian Serb forces, the appeals chamber of the ICTY ruled that *Nicaragua* set too narrow a standard and that the better test was "overall control."

Non bis in idem. Latin expression for what is known in the common law as "double jeopardy." An accused cannot be tried by a national court if he or she has already been tried by the tribunal. This also works in the other direction, but subject to important exceptions, such as sham trials held to shield someone from international prosecution. The rules are set out in article 10(2) of the statute.

Nongovernmental organizations. Among the most well-known are Amnesty International, Human Rights Watch, and the International Committee of the Red Cross. They lobby intensively for the tribunal to work effectively, adopting the view that international prosecution is an effective way to promote human rights and international humanitarian law.

Noninternational armed conflict. In popular parlance, a civil war. But international humanitarian law takes care to distinguish between noninternational armed conflict and situations of internal disturbances and tensions, such as riots, isolated and sporadic acts of violence, or other acts of a similar nature. There may also be a requirement that there be evidence of protracted armed violence between governmental authorities and organized armed groups or between such groups within a State. Serious violations of the laws or customs of war committed during noninternational armed conflict include violations of common Article 3 of the Geneva Conventions, as well as some serious violations of Additional Protocol II. They are punishable under the ICTY Statute. A noninternational armed conflict may become "internationalized" if another state intervenes in that conflict through its troops or, alternatively, if some of the participants in the internal armed conflict act on behalf of that other state.

Notice of appeal. Written declaration, filed within fifteen days of judgment, indicating a party's intent to appeal.

Nullum crimen sine lege. Latin for, literally, "no crime without law." This is the prohibition of retroactive crimes. Nothing explicit in the statute gives the tribunal the right to apply this rule. But the judges refuse to *interpret* provisions in a way that might be inconsistent with what was recognized to be the state of the law when the crime was committed.

Office of the Prosecutor. The organ within the ICTY that is responsible for preparing prosecutions and presenting them to the Tribunal at trial. It includes units dealing with investigation, research, and prosecution itself. The Office of the Prosecutor is headed by the prosecutor, Carla Del Ponte, and the deputy prosecutor, Graham Blewitt.

Official position. Official position is not a defense. In the past, tyrants alleged that they were merely acting on behalf of a state and that they could not be held responsible individually for criminal offenses. The *Pinochet* judgment of the English House of Lords rejected this view, but it was already set out clearly in the statute of the ICTY, which says official position "shall not relieve such person of criminal responsibility nor mitigate punishment."

Opening statements. Before presentation of evidence by the prosecutor, each party may make an opening statement. The defense may, however, elect to make its statement after the conclusion of the prosecutor's presentation of evidence and before the presentation of evidence for the defense.

Order. A ruling by a judge or a trial chamber that relates to the preparation of the trial, transfer of suspects, protection of witnesses, provisional release of an accused on bail, and similar matters. In August 2001 the trial chamber issued an order to the Registrar (see Registry) concerning designation of *amici curiae* for the Milosevic trial. An order may even be directed to a state to obtain documents in its possession. A ruling that does not order anything may be called a "decision". In certain limited circumstances, the registrar may also make orders and decisions.

Ordinary crime. The crime underlying an international crime, for example, the crime of killing that underlies the crime of genocide or grave breaches of the Geneva Convention. The Prosecutor must establish the commission of the ordinary crime but also must prove the special elements that make it rise to the level of an international crime, such as genocidal intent or the existence of an International armed conflict. The tribunal has reserved the right, as an exception to the double jeopardy rule, to prosecute someone who has already been convicted by a national court of the "ordinary crime" that is subsumed within the international crime.

Pardon. An executive act that cancels a conviction and leads to the release of the convict. The tribunal cannot grant one, but because detention of prisoners is served in penitentiaries of other states, their governments can.

Persecution. A crime against humanity consisting of the deprivation of fundamental rights. These are acts that are not inherently criminal but that may nonetheless become criminal and persecutorial if committed on political, racial, and religious grounds. Milosevic faces charges of persecution with respect to all three of the Indictments.

Personal jurisdiction. Sometimes criminal legislation specifies that courts have jurisdiction over crimes committed by their citizens or, more rarely, committed against their citizens. But there is nothing of the sort in the Statute of the ICTY. Anyone who commits a crime on the territory of the former Yugoslavia is, theoretically, subject to the tribunal's jurisdiction. The statute ought to have set an age limit in order to ensure that juveniles or children could not be punished. The idea doesn't seem to have occurred to the Security Council and, if the experience of eight years of prosecution is any indication, the prosecutor has shown no interest in going after teenagers, at one end of the spectrum, or, for that matter, the elderly, at the other. In legal Latin, *ratione personae* jurisdiction.

Plunder. Archaic term used to describe appropriation of property by force during armed conflict.

Precedent. A previous decision of a court that resolves a legal issue. The trial chambers are bound to follow the law set out in decisions of the appeals chambers but need not follow those of other trial chambers. Judgments of post–World War II war crimes tribunals, international judicial bodies like the International Court of Justice and the European Court of Human Rights, and even rulings of national courts are regularly invoked by the judges of the ICTY as they interpret the statute.

Preliminary motion. An application to the tribunal by one of the parties made prior to the trial itself in order to resolve issues that affect the future proceedings, such as the joinder of defendants or details about the indictment.

President. The president of the ICTY is elected by the judges. The president presides at plenary meetings of the tribunal's judges, coordinates the work of the chambers, and supervises the activities of the registry. The current president is Claude Jorda. Previous presidents were Antonio Cassese and Gabrielle Kirk McDonald. The president is assisted by a vice-president.

Presiding Judge. Each of the trial chambers elects a presiding judge. He or she directs the proceedings and has some limited functions with respect to matters such as language of the proceedings and disqualification of judges.

Pretrial brief, see Trial brief.

Pretrial judge. A member of the trial chambers that will hear the case who is designated by the presiding judge to oversee the disclosure of evidence and the preparation and submission of pretrial briefs.

Prima facie. Latin expression indicating that there is sufficiently credible evidence to sustain a conviction if not contradicted by the accused. At the time of issuance of an indictment, the reviewing judge must determine that the material facts alleged in the indictment establish a *prima facie* case and that there is evidence available which supports those material facts. During the trial, if the defense makes a motion to acquit at the end of the prosecution's evidence, the trial chamber must grant the motion if the prosecution has not made out a *prima facie* case.

Primacy, see Concurrent jurisdiction.

Prisoner of war. A prisoner of war is a captured enemy combatant who wears a distinctive sign, carries arms openly, and does not violate the laws or customs of war. Prisoner-of-war status is presumed upon capture but may be contested before a court. Prisoners-of-war status is regulated by the third Geneva Convention of 1949.

Proprio motu. Latin for "on its own initiative." In an adversarial system, like that of the common law and, in a general sense, of the ICTY, the initiative is left to the prosecution and to the defense. But in some cases, the judges may intervene *proprio motu* even where the defense and the prosecutor are silent. For example, the trial chamber may, on its own initiative, issue such orders, summonses, subpoenas, warrants, and transfer orders as may be necessary for the purposes of an investigation or for the preparation or conduct of the trial. Broad *proprio motu* powers make the ICTY rather more of a hybrid between the adversarial system of the common law and the inquisitorial system of continental European justice systems.

Prosecutor, see Office of the Prosecutor.

Protected person. Categories of persons protected by the Geneva Conventions, namely, former combatants who can no longer fight because they are wounded or taken prisoner and civilians. Grave breaches of the Geneva Conventions, other serious violations of the Geneva Conventions, and violations of Common Article 3 of the Geneva Conventions must be committed against such protected persons.

Protocols Additional, see Additional Protocols.

Provisional measures. The tribunal may order provisional measures so as to freeze the assets of an accused. These are directed to governments and have two objectives: to facilitate granting restitution of property or payment from its proceeds and to prevent an accused who is still at large from using those assets to evade arrest or to disguise assets, putting them beyond the reach of the tribunal. Upon issuance of the first indictment against Milosevic, in May 1999, Judge David Hunt ordered all members states of the United Nations to make inquiries to discover whether Milosevic had assets located in their territory. If so, they were to adopt provisional measures to freeze these assets.

Racial group. Archaic term used to describe what we now know as "Ethnic groups." One of the four groups protected by the prohibition of genocide.

Rape. All of the crimes within the jurisdiction of the ICTY can be committed by the underlying act of rape. There is no international definition of rape, so the tribunal has attempted to distill the various definitions from national legal systems. It considers that rape involves nonconsensual sexual penetration of the vagina or anus of the victim by the penis of the perpetrator or any other object; or sexual penetration of the mouth of the victim by the penis of the perpetrator. The offender must intend to effect the sexual penetration and know that it occurs without the consent of the victim. Although there is much evidence of systematic rapes being committed by Serb forces during the conflicts, Milosevic has not been charged with rape.

Rebuttal. When the defense has closed its case, the prosecutor is entitled to rebut the case by introducing a limited amount of new evidence to answer new matters that arose from the defense evidence and that it could not reasonably have anticipated.

Record on appeal. The appeal is not a new trial and as a general rule it does not consider evidence that was not initially presented to the trial chamber during the trial. The appeals chamber bases its decision exclusively on the "record on appeal," consisting of transcripts of the testimony at the trial, documents and other material evidence entered into evidence, and the various written proceedings of the court file.

Recusal, see Disqualification.

Registry. Organ of the ICTY responsible for administration and servicing of the other two organs of the tribunal, the chambers and the office of the prosecutor. The trial chamber assigned to the Milosevic case has issued an order that invites the registrar to designate *amici curiae* to assist in the case. The head of the registry, the registrar, is appointed by the secretary-general of the United Nations. Currently, the registrar is Hans Holthuis.

Rejoinder. Prosecution evidence that is introduced in "Rebuttal," that is, to answer the defense case, may itself be contested by the defense with the production of "rejoinder" evidence. But the defense cannot use this as a chance to raise entirely new issues or produce evidence that it had neglected to present earlier in the trial.

Religious group. A group protected by the prohibition of genocide. Intentional destruction of a religious group is a form of genocide. The category was included in the prohibition to ensure that disputes as to whether Jews or Muslims, for example, were not an ethnic but rather a religious group would not provide a loophole for defendants.

Restitution. Return of property and its proceeds to the rightful owner. After a judgment of conviction, the trial chamber shall hold a special hearing to determine whether property should be restituted. Because this may affect the rights of third parties, they may participate in the proceedings and make their own claims to possession or ownership.

Review. Aside from a genuine appeal, which both defense and prosecution may file in order to challenge errors of law and fact made by the trial chamber, both sides may also seek review of a final judgment where a new fact has been discovered which was not known to them at the time of the proceedings and that could not have been discovered through the exercise of due diligence. The defense can do this at any time, but the prosecutor can seek review only within one year of the judgment.

Reviewing judge. Judge of the ICTY responsible for authorizing the issuance of an indictment. In the Milosevic case, the reviews were conducted by Judge David Hunt.

Romano-Germanic system. A system of criminal procedure widely used in continental Europe and other parts of the world, sometimes also called the "civil law system" or the "inquisitorial system." Unlike the common law system, where this is done by prosecution and defense lawyers, it is a judge (known as the investigating or instructing magistrate) who prepares the case for trial.

Rome statute. The treaty that creates the International Criminal Court. Adopted by a diplomatic conference in July 1998, it entered into force in mid-2002, after obtaining sixty ratifications. Much like the ICTY, the court can prosecute genocide, crimes against humanity, and war crimes. It has jurisdiction over crimes committed on the territory of countries that have ratified the Rome statute or by their nationals. Croatia and the Federal Republic of Yugoslavia have ratified the Rome statute. This means that, until the Security Council puts an end to the ICTY's jurisdiction, the jurisdiction of the ICTY and the International Criminal Court considerably overlap. However, it is unlikely that the Security Council will defer the work of the ICTY to the new International Criminal Court, as some have suggested.

Rules of procedure and evidence. Detailed rules guiding the operation of the tribunal. They are adopted by the judges, under power given by article 15 of the Statute, and deal with such matters as conduct of the pretrial phase of the proceedings, trials and appeals, the admission of evidence, and the protection of victims and witnesses. They have been regularly revised by the judges over the years.

Security Council. One of the principal organs of the United Nations, with main authority over matters of international peace and security. The Security Council established the International Criminal Tribunal for the former Yugoslavia by Resolution 827, of May 25, 1993. Milosevic and others have contested whether it actually had the authority to set up such a court, but the appeals chamber, in a 1995 decision, settled this question rather decisively.

Sentence. If the tribunal decides to convict, it can impose a sentence that is limited to imprisonment. Nevertheless, any evidence or arguments that the defense wishes to submit in order to mitigate sentence must be produced during the trial itself, before the trial chamber has ruled on the issue of guilt.

Severance. Where an Indictment deals with two or more accused persons, it may be necessary to "sever" the cases of specific defendants in order to ensure a fair trial. Severance may also occur if an indictment deals with two or more quite separate and distinct fact situations, with no obvious relationship between them.

Statute. The legal basis for the operations of the ICTY. It is annexed to Security Council Resolution 827. The Statute provides only summary direction to the tribunal and has been completed with considerably greater detail in the rules of procedure and evidence, which are adopted by the judges themselves.

Subject matter jurisdiction. The crimes which the ICTY is empowered to try, namely, grave breaches of the Geneva Conventions, violations of the laws or customs of war, genocide, and crimes against humanity. In legal Latin, *ratione materiae* jurisdiction.

Subordinate, see Command responsibility.

Subpoena. An order issued by a judge or a trial chamber directing a person to testify in person or to produce a document that is under their control.

Superior responsibility, see Command responsibility.

Superior orders. A classic defense in war crimes trials, in which the obedient soldier admits committing a war crime but says, "I was only following orders." Even in post–World War I trials, superior orders was rejected as a defense in cases where the order was manifestly unlawful. To avoid any debate on this point, the ICTY statute simply prohibits the defense (see article 7[4]). But the Tribunal can take the issue into account in mitigation of punishment.

Suspect. A person concerning whom the prosecutor possesses reliable information that tends to show that the person may have committed a crime over which the tribunal has jurisdiction.

***Tadic* decision.** Shorthand reference by insiders to an important ruling by the appeals chamber, in October 1995, that established that the tribunal was created properly by the Security Council, and that violations of the laws or customs of war could be committed during noninternational armed conflict.

Temporal jurisdiction. The tribunal can punish only crimes committed within its temporal jurisdiction, that is, since January 1, 1991. The temporal jurisdiction will come to an end when the Security Council so decides, but it has thus far done nothing, and so the tribunal continues to have authority to prosecute crimes committed to this day. In legal Latin, this is *ratione temporis* jurisdiction.

Territorial jurisdiction. The tribunal can punish only crimes committed within its territorial jurisdiction, that is, the territory of the former Yugoslavia, including its land surface, airspace and territorial waters. This includes not only modern-day Croatia, Bosnia and Herzegovina, and the Federal Republic of Yugoslavia, for which there are Indictments, but also Macedonia and Slovenia, for which there are not. An unresolved question is whether the tribunal can also punish behavior outside the borders of the former Yugoslavia but which has direct effects on its territory. The tribunal also exercises jurisdiction over some offenses committed at its seat in The Hague, namely, contempt of court and perjury.

Torture. Torture can be prosecuted as a grave breach of the Geneva Conventions, a serious violation of the laws or customs of war, or a crime against humanity. It consists of the intentional infliction of severe pain or suffering, whether physical or mental, upon a person in the custody or under the control of the accused. Torture must be conducted for a prohibited purpose, such as obtaining information or a confession, punishing, intimidating, humiliating, or coercing the victim or a third person or discriminating, on any ground, against the victim or a third person.

Transaction. A number of acts or omissions, whether occurring as one event or a number of events, at the same or different locations, and being part of a common scheme, strategy, or plan.

Transfer. The ICTY statute uses the word *transfer* to describe what in the context of a National criminal justice system is called "extradition." But the ICTY is not a state, so *extradition* is not the right word for surrender of an offender. Milosevic was transferred to the ICTY from the Federal Republic of Yugoslavia in June 2001. He has claimed that the transfer was not consistent with the laws of Yugoslavia, but this issue is of little concern to the ICTY, and the argument was dismissed in a November 2001 pretrial ruling.

Trial brief. Both prosecutor and defense are required to set out their legal and factual arguments in writing. First, they must submit a "pretrial brief," outlining the factual and legal issues, including a written statement setting out "the nature of his or her case." Then, after the evidence has been presented, both sides are also expected to present a "trial brief" prior to making their closing arguments.

Trial Chamber. Three judges of the tribunal, led by a presiding judge, who actually hear the case and rule on guilt and innocence. The trial chamber also has some responsibilities over pretrial matters.

Universal jurisdiction. As a general rule, national courts prosecute only crimes committed on their territory or by their nationals. But for certain serious crimes, of which war crimes, genocide, and crimes against humanity are the best examples, it is well recognized that any state may prosecute anyone, no matter where the crime was committed.

War crimes. This general expression refers to grave breaches of the Geneva conventions and other serious violations of the laws and customs of war. In 1995 the ICTY Appeals Chamber ruled that war crimes could be committed in noninternational armed conflict as well as in international armed conflict, a principle that was later codified in the Rome statute.

Wilful blindness. Where it is established that a defendant suspected that a fact existed, or was aware that its existence was highly probable but refrained from finding out whether it did exist so as to be able to deny knowledge, this is deemed to be equivalent to real knowledge for the purpose of establishing the mental element or *Mens rea* of the offense.

BIBLIOGRAPHY

Ahmed, Akbar S. "Ethnic Cleansing: A Metaphor for Our Time." In *The Conceit of Innocence: Losing the Conscience of the West in the War against Bosnia*, ed. Stjepan G. Meštovic. College Station: Texas A&M University Press, 1997.

Almond, Mark. *Europe's Backyard War: The War in the Balkans*. London: Mandarin, 1994.

Arendt, Hanna. *Eichmann in Jerusalem: A Report on the Banality of Evil*. New York: Penguin USA, 1963.

Bass, Gary. *Stay the Hand of Vengeance: The Politics of War Crimes Tribunals*. Princeton, N.J.: Princeton University Press, 2000.

Bassiouni, M. Cherif, and Peter Manikas. *The Law of the International Criminal Tribunal for the former Yugoslavia*. Irvington-on-Hudson, N.Y.: Transnational, 1996.

Bennett, Christopher. *Yugoslavia's Bloody Collapse: Causes, Course and Consequence*. New York: New York University Press, 1996.

Bildt, Carl. *Peace Journey: The Struggle for Peace in Bosnia*. Weinfield, London: Orion, 1998.

Boyle, Francis Anthony. *The Bosnian People Charge Genocide*. Northampton, Mass.: Aletheia, 1996.

Burg, Steven, and Paul Shoup. *The War in Bosnia-Herzegovina: Ethnic Conflict and International Intervention*. London: M.E. Sharpe, 1998.

Campbell, David. *National Deconstruction: Violence, Identity and Justice in Bosnia.* Minneapolis: University of Minnesota Press, 1998.

Ceh, Nick, and Jeff Harder (ed.). *The Golden Apple: Wars and Democracy in Croatia and Bosnia.* Boulder, Colo.: Eastern European Monographs, 1996.

Chayes, Abram, and Antonia Handler Chayes. "After the End." In *The World and Yugoslavia's Wars,* ed. Richard H. Ullman. New York: Council on Foreign Relations, 1996.

Clark, Roger S., and Madeleine Sann (ed.). *The Prosecution of International War Crimes.* New Brunswick, N.J.: Transaction, 1996

Cohen, Lenard. *Broken Bonds: Yugoslavia's Disintegration and Balkan Politics in Transition.* Boulder, Colo.: Westview Press, 1995.

————. *Serpent in the Bosom: The Rise and Fall of Slobodan Milosevic.* Boulder, Colo.: Westview Press, 2000.

Cohen, Roger. *Hearts Grown Brutal: Sagas of Sarajevo.* New York: Random House, 1998.

Cooper, Belinda. *War Crimes: The Legacy of Nuremberg.* With a forward by Richard J. Goldstone. New York: TV Books, 1999.

Denitch, Bogdan. *Ethnic Nationalism: The Tragic Death of Yugoslavia,* 3rd ed. Minneapolis: University of Minnesota Press, 1996.

Dinstein, Yoram, and Mala Tabory (ed.). *War Crimes in International Law.* The Hague: Martinus Nijhoff, 1996.

Doder, Dusko, and Louise Branson. *Milosevic: Portrait of a Tyrant.* New York: Free Press, 1999.

Donia, Robert, and John Fine. *Bosnia-Hercegovina: A Tradition Betrayed.* London: Columbia University Press, 1994.

Dragnitch, Alex. *Serbs and Croats: The Struggle in Yugoslavia.* New York: Harcourt Brace, 1992.

Friedman, Francine. *The Bosnian Muslims: Denial of a Nation.* Boulder, Colo.: Westview Press, 1996.

Gagnon, Jr., V. P. "Historical Roots of the Yugoslav Conflict." In *International Organization and Ethnic Conflict,* ed. Milton J.

Esman and Shelby Telhami. Ithaca, N.Y.: Cornell University Press, 1995.

Glenny, Misha. *The Fall of Yugoslavia: The Third Balkan War.* London: Viking Penguin, 1992.

Goldstone, Richard. *For Humanity: Reflections of a War Crimes Investigator.* New Haven: Yale University Press, 2000.

Gutman, Roy. *Witness to Genocide.* New York: Macmillan, 1993.

Gutman, Roy, and David Rieff. *Crimes of War: What the Public Should Know.* London: W.W. Norton, 1999.

Holbrooke, Richard. *To End a War.* New York: Random House, 1999.

Honig, Jan Willem, and Norbert Both. *Srebrenica: Record of a War Crime.* London: Viking Penguin, 1996.

Horowitz, Donald K. *Ethnic Groups in Conflict.* Berkeley and Los Angeles: University of California Press, 1985.

Hosmer, Stephen T. *The Conflict over Kosovo: Why Milosevic Decided to Settle When He Did.* C. Hurst, 1998.

Jelavich, Barbara. *History of the Balkans.* Cambridge, England: Cambridge University Press, 1983.

Jones, R. W .D. *The Practice of the International Criminal Tribunals for the Former Yugoslavia and Rwanda.* Irvington-on-Hudson, N.Y.: Transnational, 1998.

Judah, Tim. *The Serbs: History, Myth and the Destruction of Yugoslavia.* New Haven: Yale University Press, 1997.

Lampe, John. *Yugoslavia as History: Twice There Was a Country.* Cambridge: England, Cambridge University Press, 1996.

Lescure, Karine, and Florence Trintignac. *International Justice for Former Yugoslavia: The Workings of the International Criminal Tribunal.* The Hague: Kluwer Law International, 1996.

Magas, Branka. *The Destruction of Yugoslavia: Tracking the Breakup, 1980–92.* London: New Left Books, 1993.

Malcolm, Noel. *Bosnia: A Short History.* New York: New York University Press, 1994.

McCormack, Timothy I. H., and Gerry Simpson (ed.). *The Law of War Crimes: National and International Approaches.* The Hague: Kluwer Law International, 1997.

Metrovic, Stjepan G. *The Conceit of Innocence: Losing the Conscience of the West in the War against Bosnia.* College Station: Texas A&M University Press, 1997.

Minow, Martha. *Between Vengeance and Forgiveness: Facing History after Genocide and Mass Violence.* Boston: Beacon Press, 1998.

Mousavizadeh, Nader (ed.). *The Black Book of Bosnia: The Consequences of Appeasement.* New York: Perseus Books, 1995.

Neier, Aryeh. *War Crimes: Brutality, Genocide, Terror and the Struggle for Justice.* New York: Random House, 1998.

Neuffer, Elizabeth. *The Key to My Neighbor's House: Seeking Justice in Bosnia and Rwanda.* New York: Picador, 2001.

O'Ballance, Edgar. *Civil War in Bosnia, 1992–94.* London: St. Martin's Press, 1995.

Pavkovic, Aleksandar. *The Fragmentation of Yugoslavia: Nationalism in a Multi-National State.* London: Macmillan, 1997.

Pešic, Vesna. *Serbian Nationalism and the Origins of the Yugoslav Crisis.* Washington, D.C.: United States Institute of Peace, 1996.

Power, Samantha. *Breakdown in the Balkans: A Chronicle of Events January 1989 to May 1993.* Washington D.C., 1993.

Ramcharan, B. G. (ed.). *The International Conference on the Former Yugoslavia: Official Papers.* Dordrecht, the Netherlands: Kluwer Law International, 1997.

Rezun, Miron. *Europe and War in the Balkans: Towards a New Yugoslav Identity.* Westport, Conn.: Praeger, 1995.

Rogel, Carole. *The Breakup of Yugoslavia and the War in Bosnia.* Westport, Conn.: Praeger, 1998.

Schabas, William A. *Genocide in International Law.* Cambridge, England: Cambridge University Press, 2000.

———. *Introduction to the International Criminal Court.* Cambridge, England: Cambridge University Press, 2001.

Scharf, Michael P. *Balkan Justice: The Story behind the First International War Crimes Tribunal since Nuremberg.* Durham, N.C.: Carolina Academic Press, 1997.

———. *The Law of International Organizations.* Durham, N.C.: Carolina Academic Press, 2001.

Scharf, Michael P., and Virginia Morris. *An Insider's Guide to the International Criminal Tribunal for the Former Yugoslavia.* New York: Transnational, 1995.

Stojanovic, Svetozar. *The Fall of Yugoslavia.* New York: Prometheus Books, 1997.

Stewart, Colonel Bob. *Broken Lives: A Personal View of the Bosnian Conflict.* New York: HarperCollins, 1994.

Tanner, Marcus. *Croatia: A Nation Forged in War.* New Haven: Yale University Press, 1997.

Taylor, Telford. *The Anatomy of the Nuremberg Trials.* New York: Aspen Law & Business, 1993.

Thomas, Robert. *Serbia under Milosevic.* Hurst, 1998.

Udovoicki, Jasminka, and James Ridgeway (ed.). *Yugoslavia's Ethnic Nightmare: The Inside Story of Europe's Unfolding Ordeal.* Chicago: Chicago Review Press, 1995.

Vulliamy, Ed. *Seasons in Hell: Understanding Bosnia's War.* New York: St. Martin's Press, 1994.

Williams, Paul, and Michael P. Scharf. *Justice with Peace? War Crimes and Accountability in the Former Yugoslavia.* Denver: Rowman and Littlefield, 2002.

Williams, Paul, Michael P. Scharf, and Dianne Orentlicher. *Making Justice Work.* New York: Century Foundation, 1998.

Woodward, Susan. *Balkan Tragedy: Chaos and Dissolution after the Cold War.* Washington, D.C.: Brookings Institution Press, 1996.